FINGER ALPHABET COOL KIDS

36
WORD SEARCH PUZZLES

WITH
THE

**AMERICAN
SIGN
LANGUAGE
ALPHABET**

VERBS

LEGENDARYMEDIA
PUBLISHING

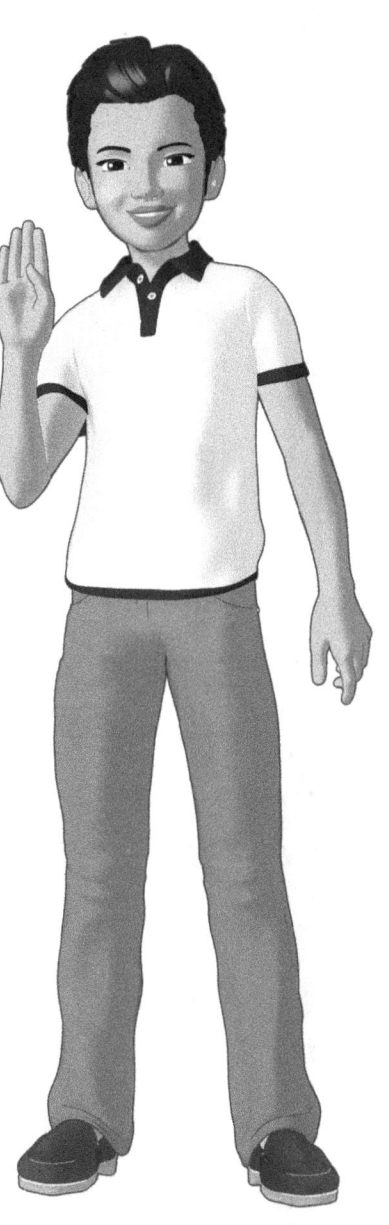

First published in 2014 by LegendaryMedia Publishing
Windmuehlstrasse 4, 60329 Frankfurt am Main, Germany

Copyright © 2014 LegendaryMedia, www.legendarymedia.de
Copyright illustrations & hand shape drawings © Lassal, www.lassal.de

All rights reserved. No part of this publication may be reproduced, stored in a retrieval system, or transmitted, in any form or by any means, electronic, mechanical, photocopying, recording or otherwise, without prior written permission by the copyright holder. Any person or persons who do any unauthorised act in relation ot this publication may be liable to criminal persecution and civil claims for damages.

ISBN: 978-3-86469-106-5
LM003-003US-VRB-E1

This book is available at quantity discounts for bulk purchases.
For information, please contact info@legendarymedia.de.

BEST PRACTICE FOR FINGERSPELLING

RIGHT HANDED PEOPLE USE RIGHT HAND

LEFT HANDED PEOPLE USE LEFT HAND

1. USE THE HAND YOU WRITE WITH
2. KEEP YOUR HAND STEADY IN ONE AREA (DO NOT BOUNCE AROUND)
3. TRY FOR A SMOOTH RHYTHM AND ACCURATE SIGNS (INSTEAD OF SPEED)
4. PAUSE BETWEEN WORDS
5. DO NOT SAY THE LETTERS WHILE FINGERSPELLING, SAY THE WORDS
6. PRACTICE, PRACTICE, PRACTICE!

REGULAR VERBS STARTING WITH "A"

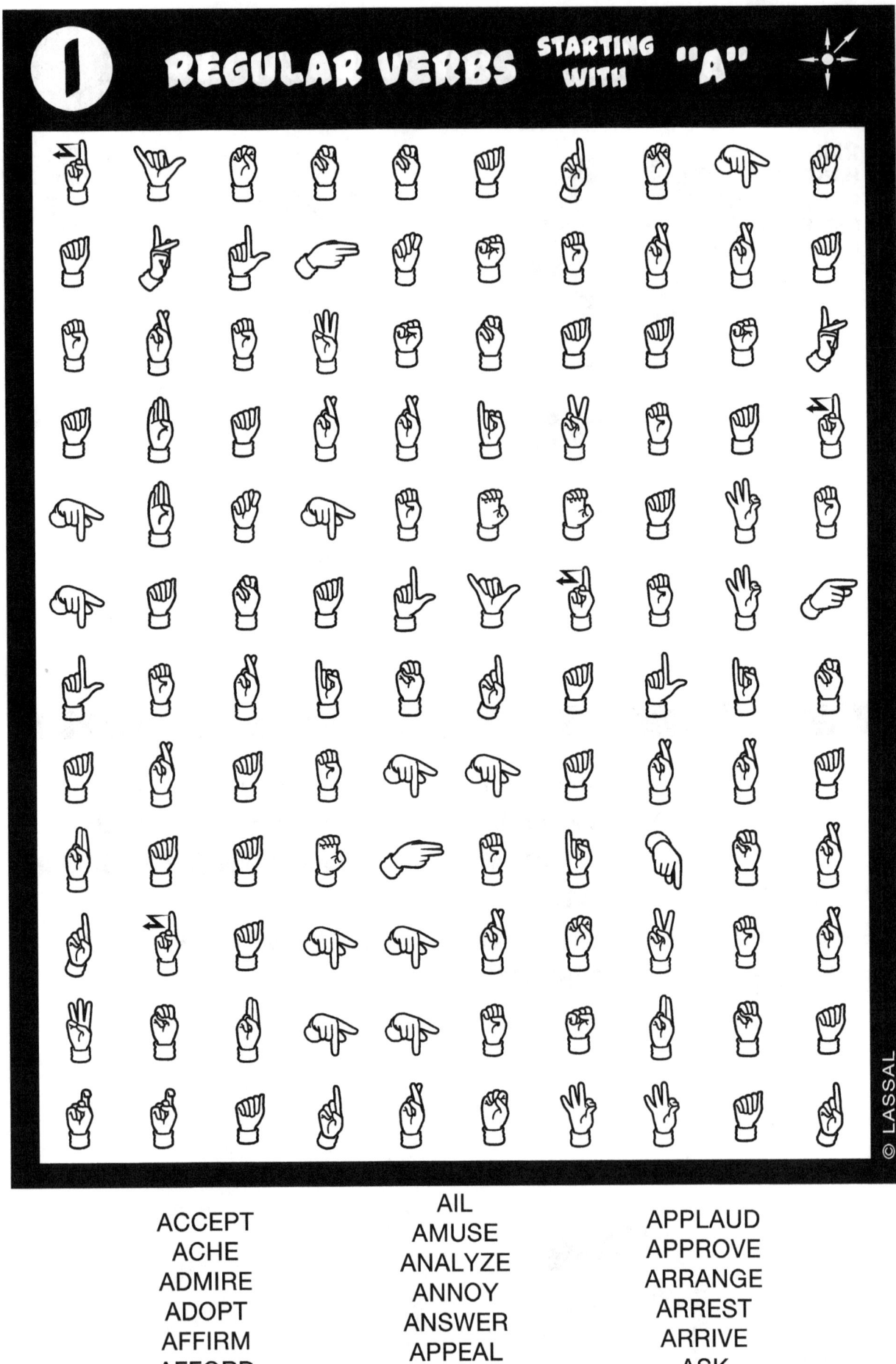

ACCEPT
ACHE
ADMIRE
ADOPT
AFFIRM
AFFORD

AIL
AMUSE
ANALYZE
ANNOY
ANSWER
APPEAL
APPEAR

APPLAUD
APPROVE
ARRANGE
ARREST
ARRIVE
ASK

REGULAR VERBS STARTING WITH "B"

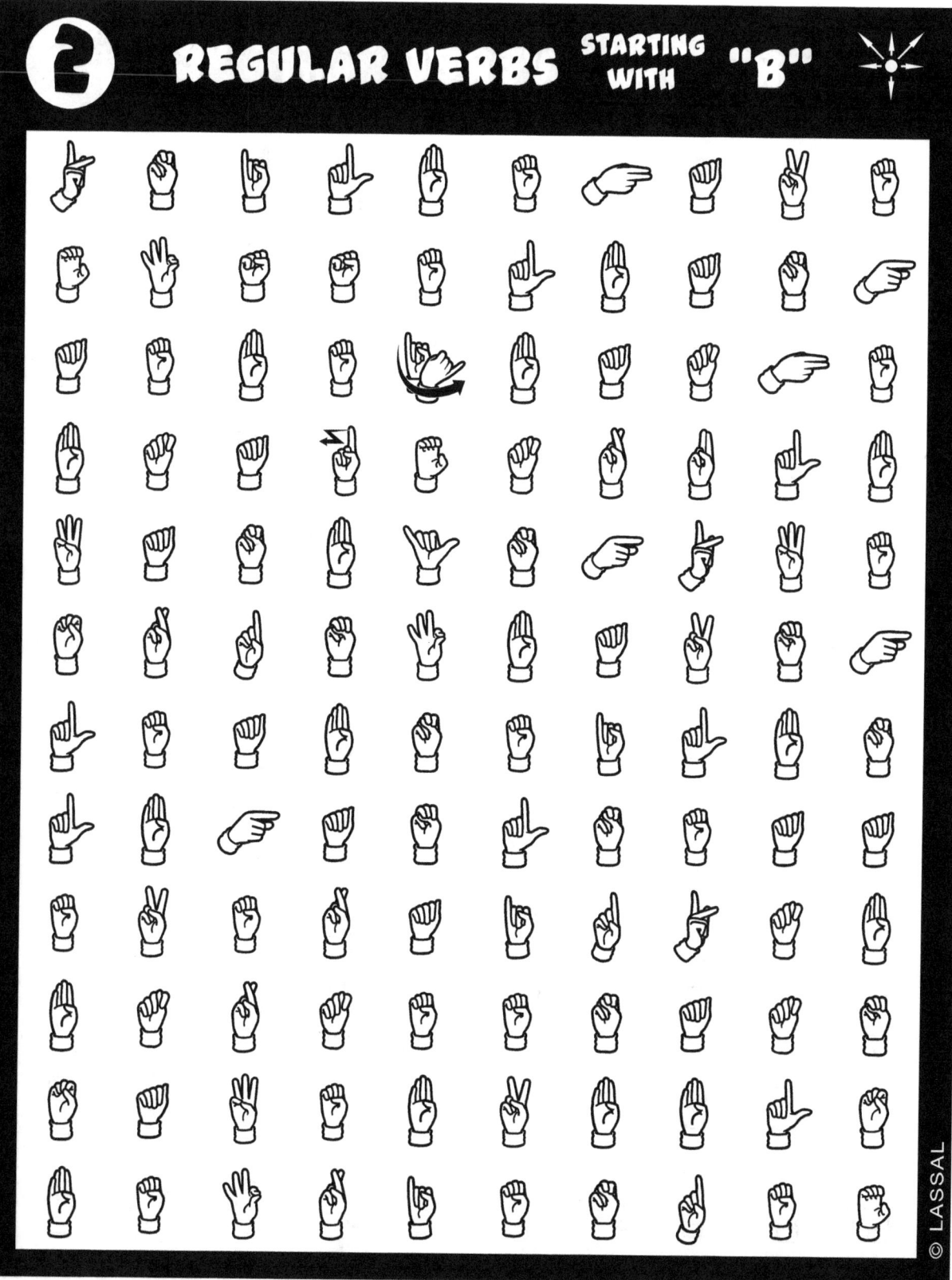

BACK	BAR	BATTLE	BELIEVE
BAKE	BARGAIN	BEAM	BELLOW
BALANCE	BARTER	BEFRIEND	BERATE
BAN	BAT	BEG	BLESS
BANG	BATHE	BEHAVE	BLINK
BANDAGE			BLURT

3 REGULAR VERBS STARTING WITH "C"

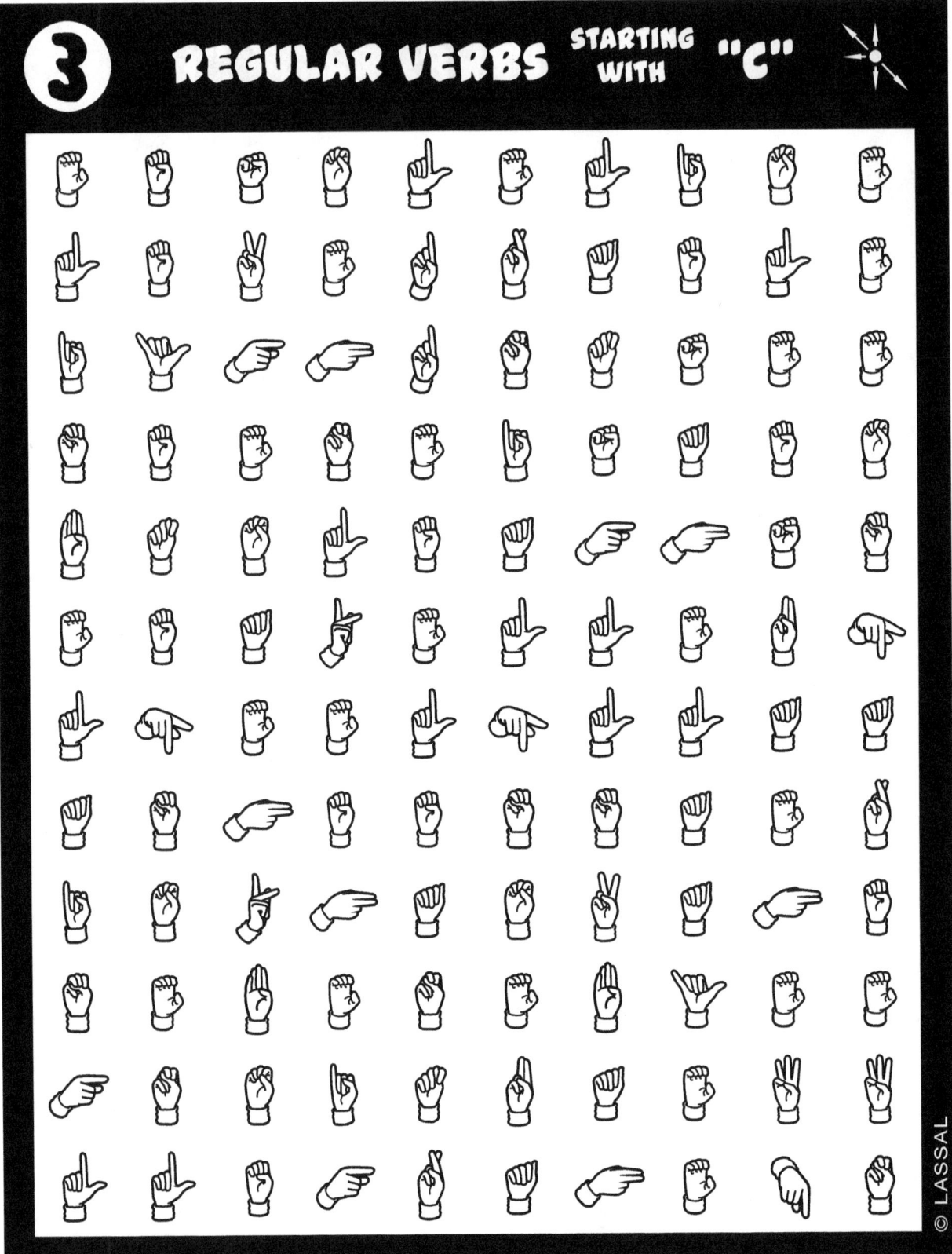

CALL	CHASE	CLOSE
CAMP	CHECK	COACH
CAUSE	CLAIM	COIL
CAUTION	CLEAN	COMPARE
CHALLENGE	CLEAR	COMPETE
CHARGE	CLIMB	COMPLAIN

4 REGULAR VERBS starting with "D"

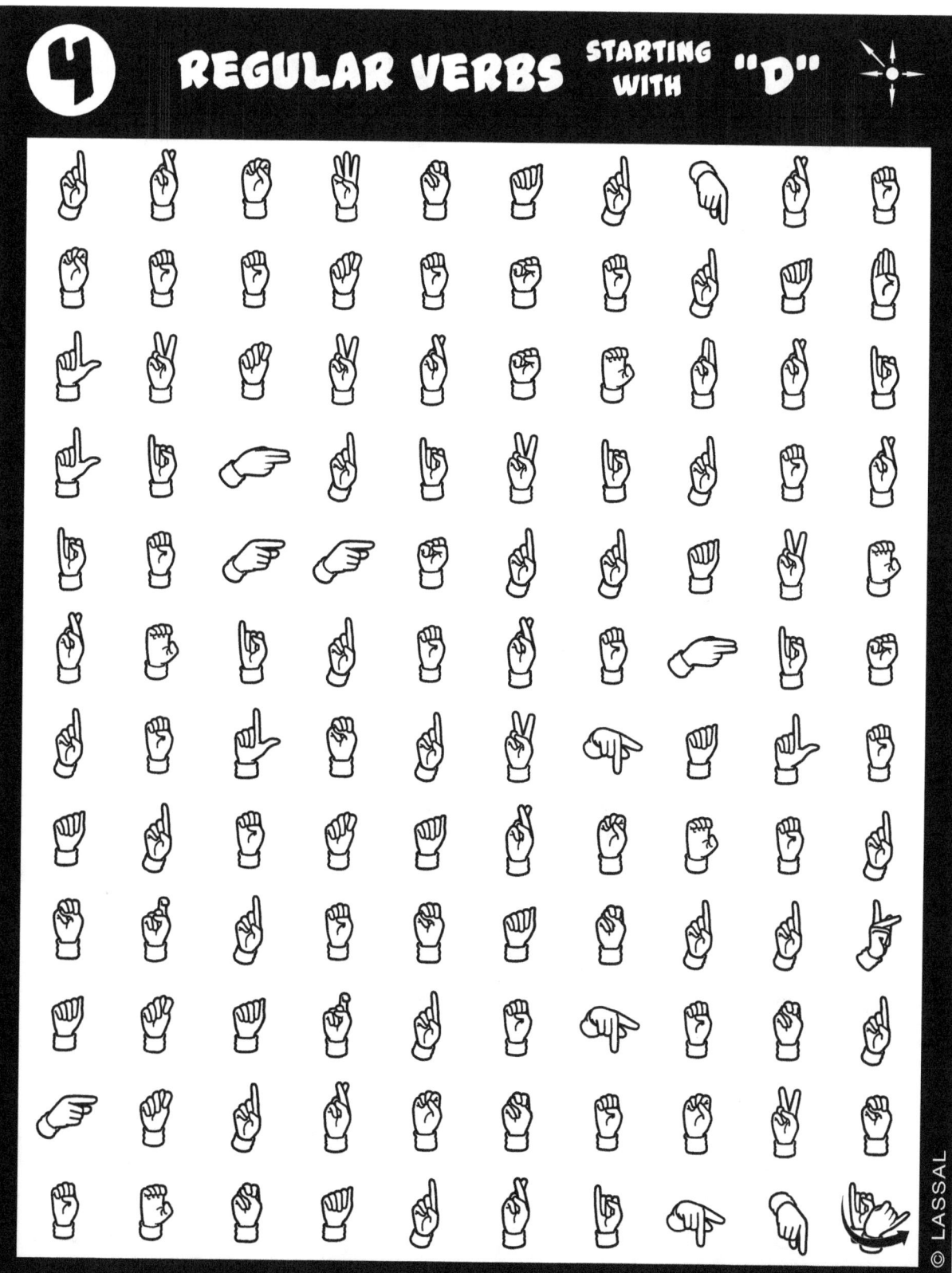

DAMAGE	DELIVER	DIVE
DANCE	DEMAND	DIVIDE
DECEIVE	DEPEND	DRIP
DECIDE	DESCRIBE	DRILL
DECORATE	DESIRE	DRONE
DELIGHT		DROWN

5 REGULAR VERBS STARTING WITH "E"

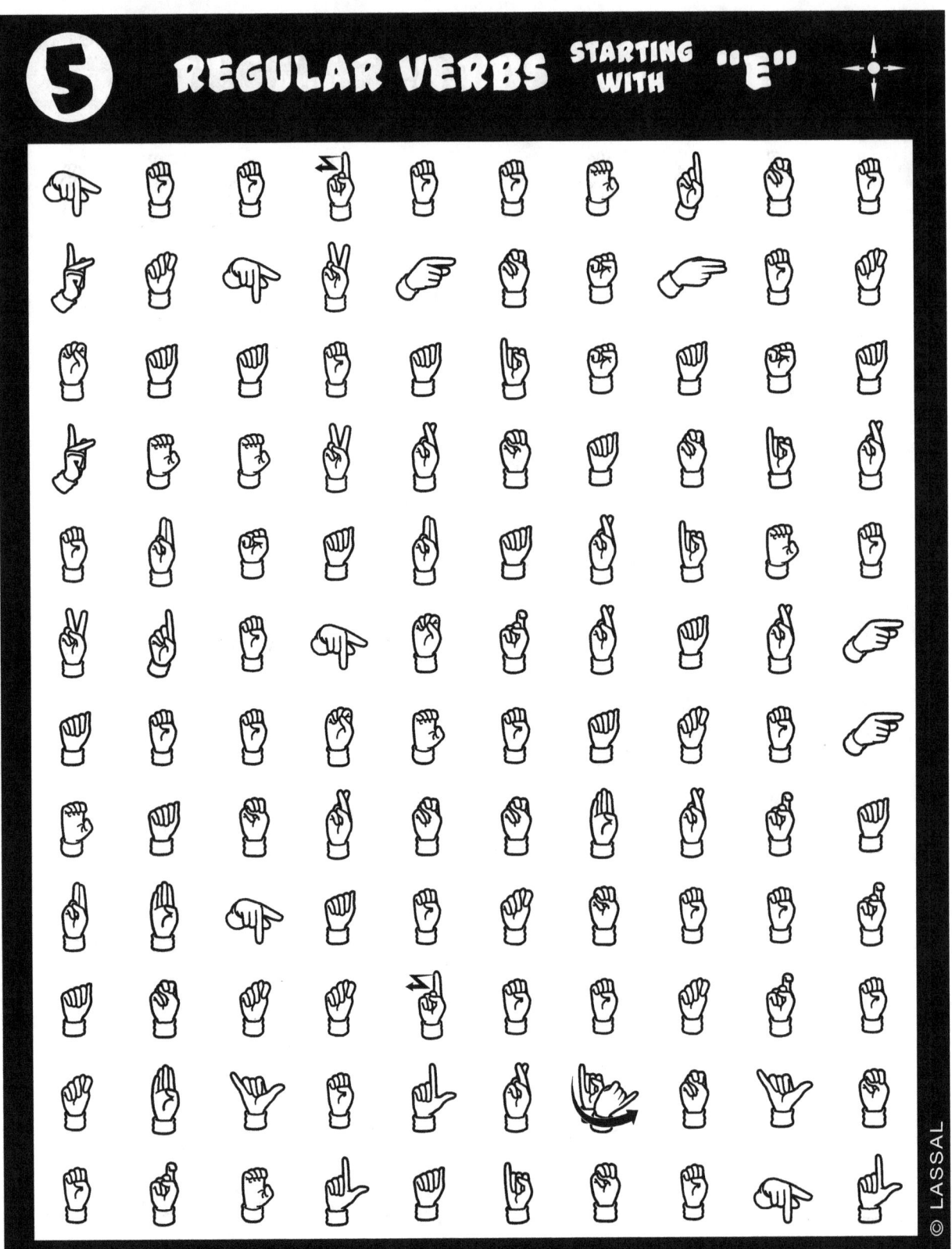

EDUCATE
EMBARRASS
EMPTY
ENCOURAGE
END

ENTER
ENTERTAIN
ESCAPE
EVACUATE

EVAPORATE
EXAGGERATE
EXAMINE
EXERCISE
EXCLAIM

6 REGULAR VERBS starting with "F"

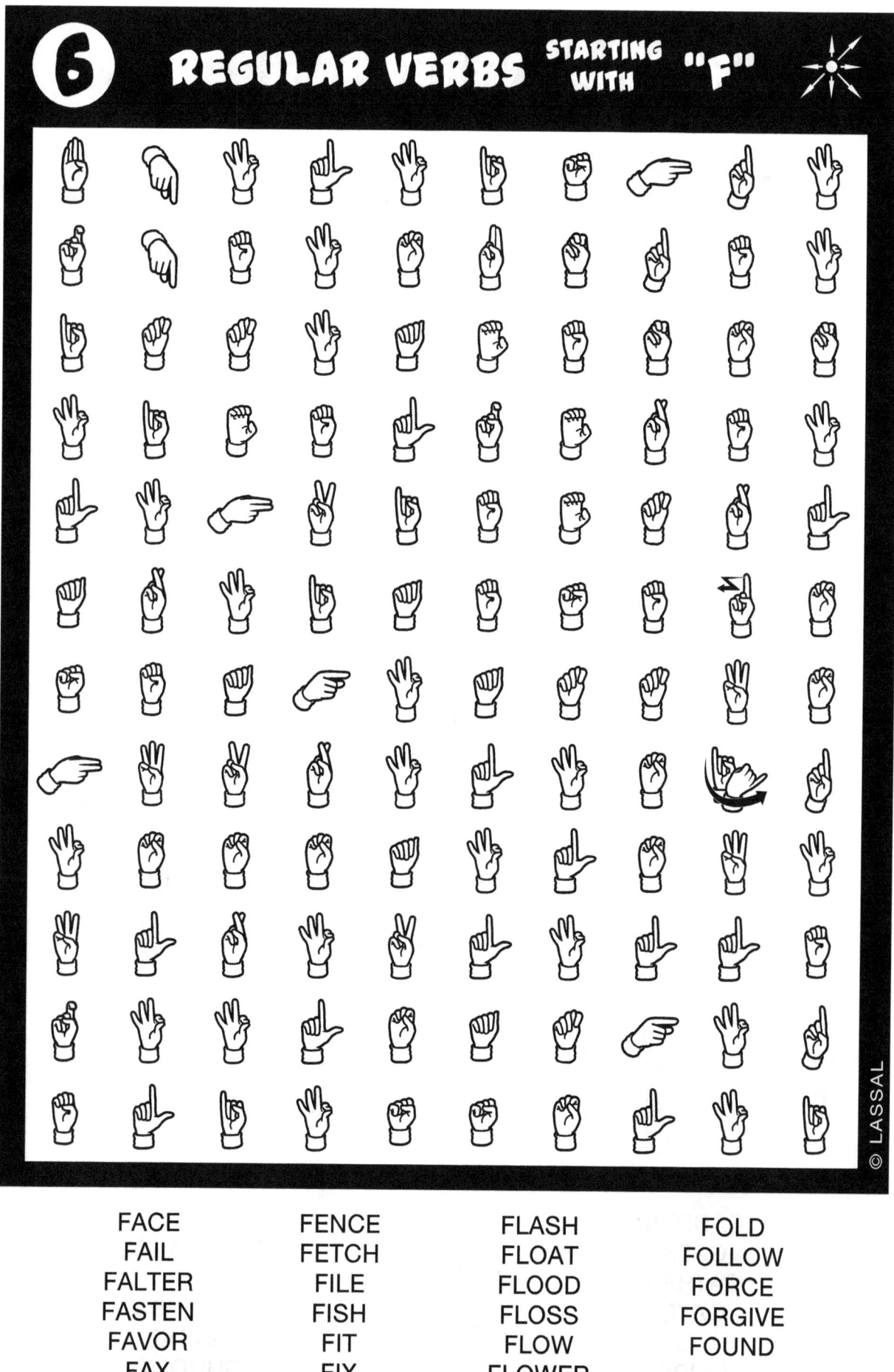

FACE	FENCE	FLASH	FOLD
FAIL	FETCH	FLOAT	FOLLOW
FALTER	FILE	FLOOD	FORCE
FASTEN	FISH	FLOSS	FORGIVE
FAVOR	FIT	FLOW	FOUND
FAX	FIX	FLOWER	

7 REGULAR VERBS STARTING WITH "G"

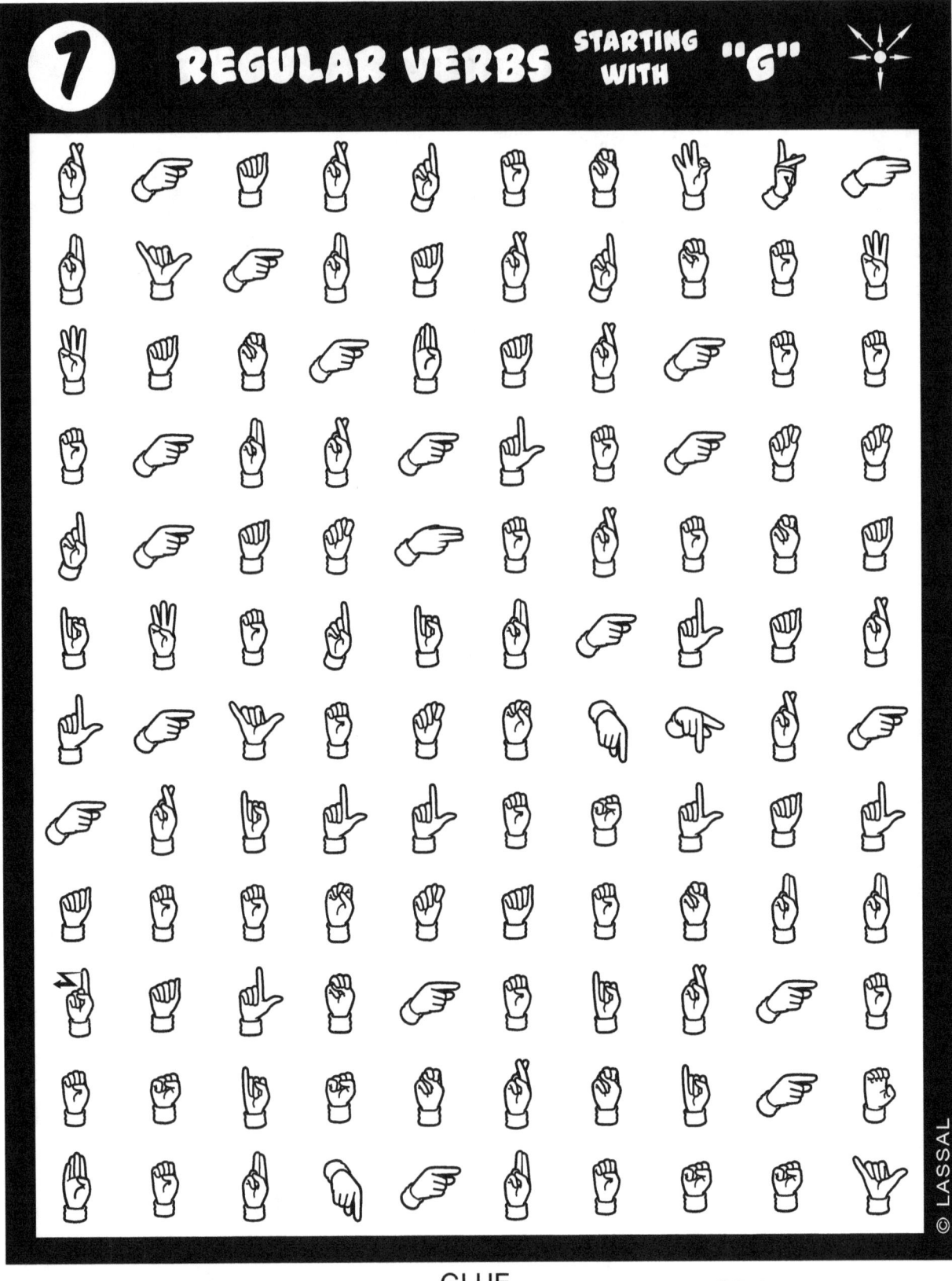

GARDEN
GASP
GATHER
GAZE
GEL
GLIDE
GLUE
GNAW
GRAB
GRATE
GREASE
GREET
GRILL
GRIN
GUARANTEE
GUARD
GUESS
GUIDE
GURGLE

REGULAR VERBS starting with "H"

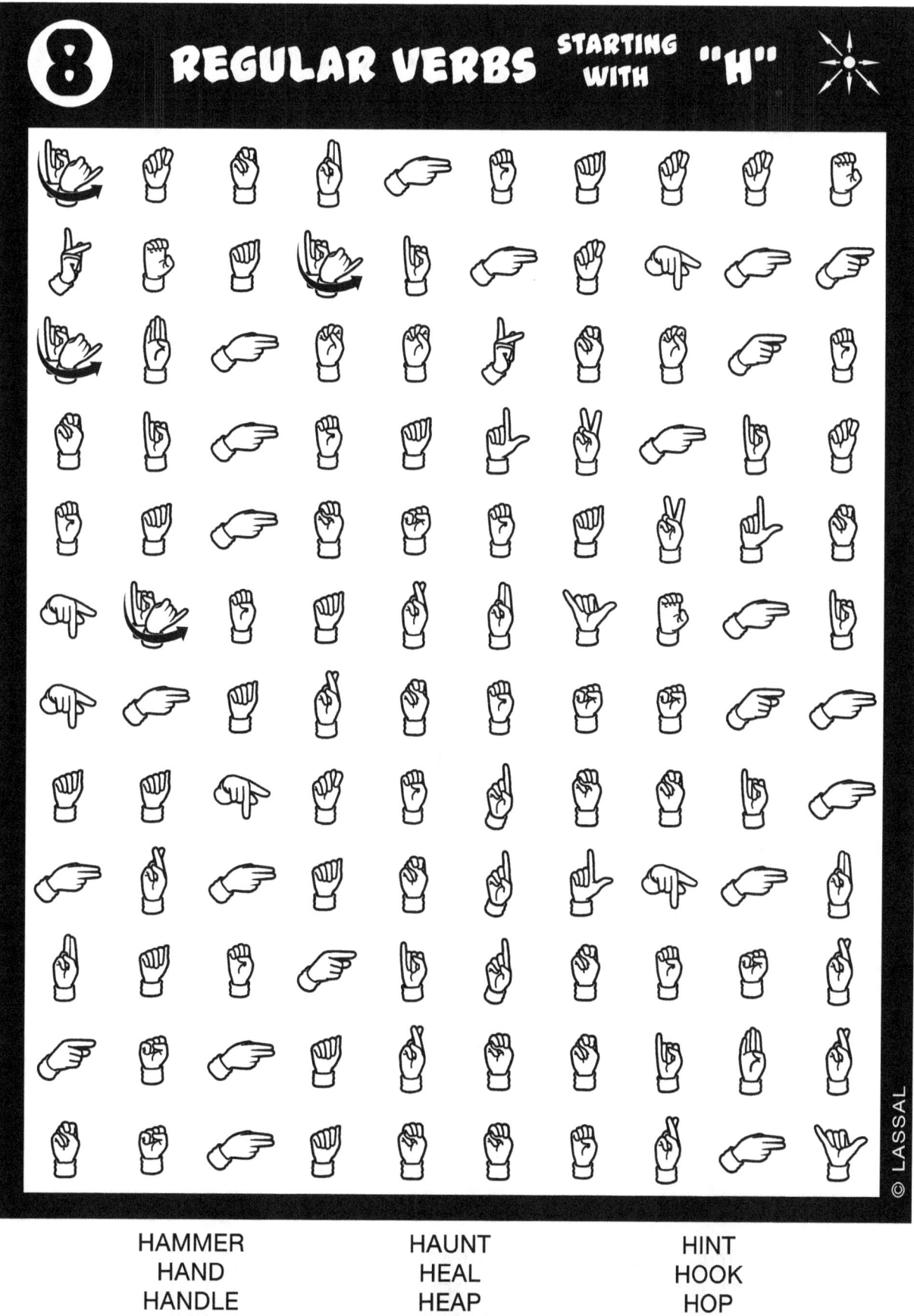

HAMMER	HAUNT	HINT
HAND	HEAL	HOOK
HANDLE	HEAP	HOP
HAPPEN	HEAT	HOVER
HARASS	HIGHLIGHT	HUG
HARM	HIJACK	HUNT
HARNESS	HINDER	HURRY

REGULAR VERBS starting with "I"

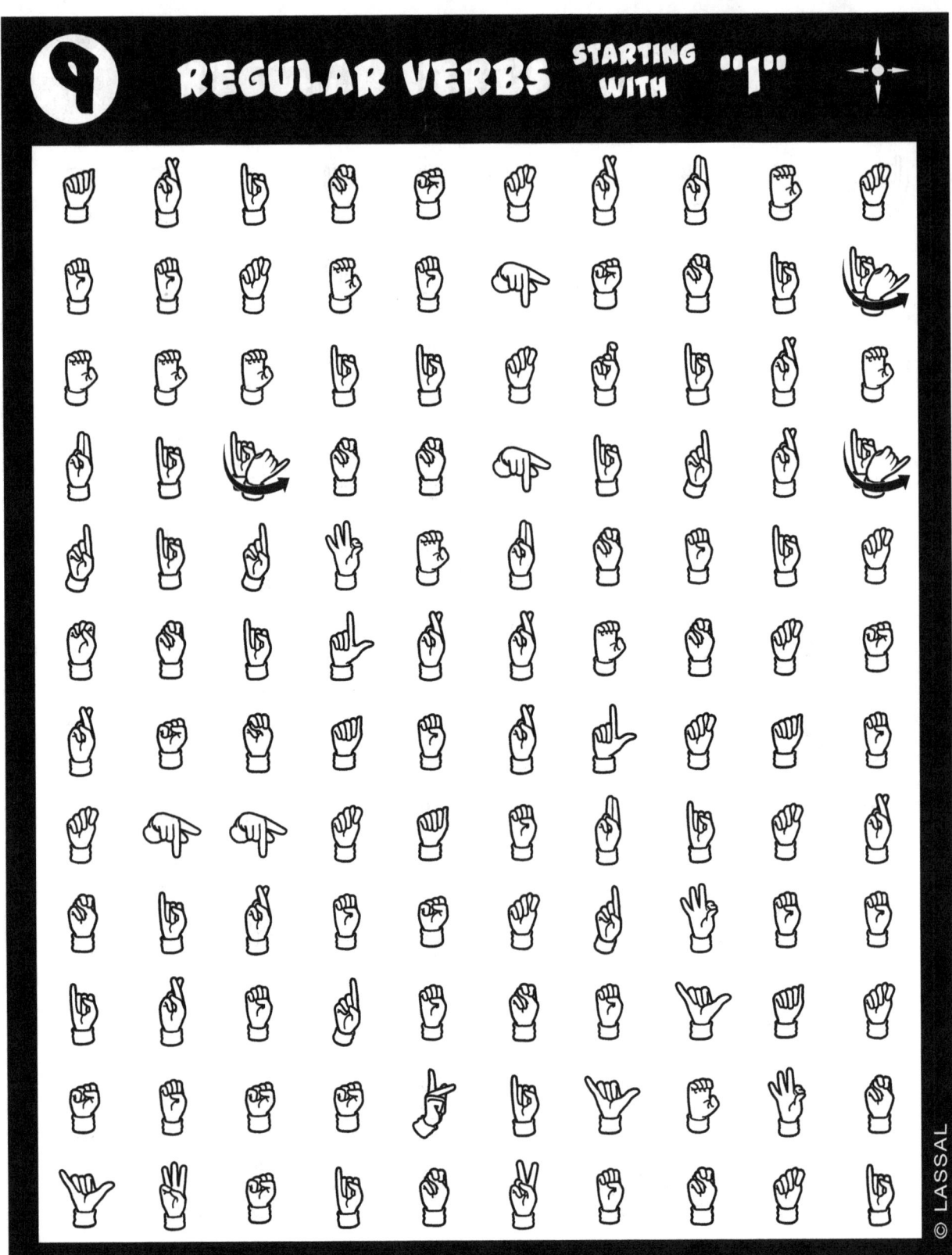

ICE	INFLATE	INTEREST
IDENTIFY	INSPECT	INTERRUPT
IMPRESS	INSPIRE	INTRODUCE
INCLUDE	INSTRUCT	INVENT
INCREASE		IRRITATE

10 REGULAR VERBS STARTING WITH "J", "K"

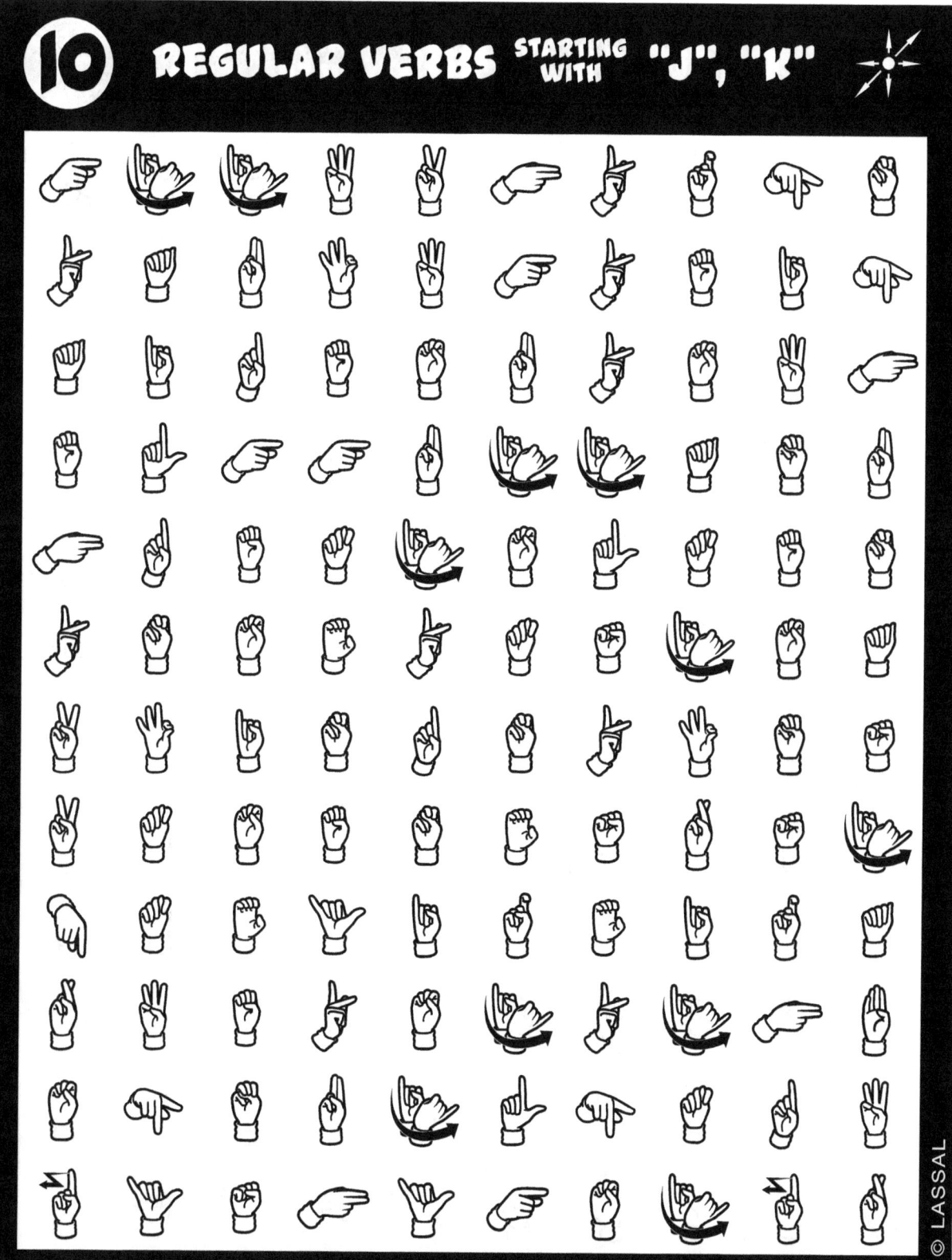

JAB	JOKE	JUMP
JAIL	JOLT	KICK
JAM	JUDGE	KISS
JOG	JUGGLE	KNOCK
JOIN		KNOT

11 REGULAR VERBS starting with "L"

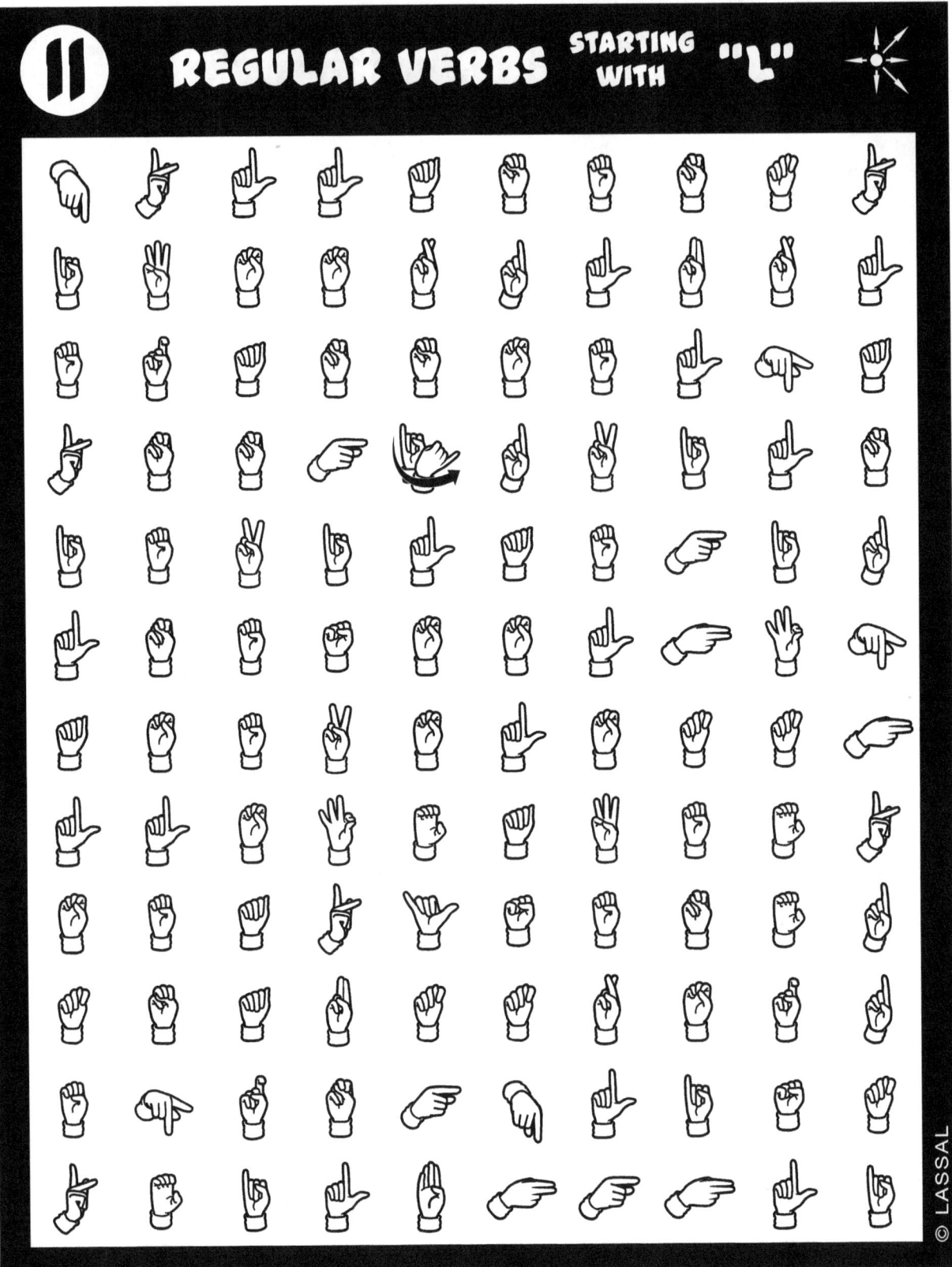

LAMENT	LIFT	LOAN
LAND	LIGHTEN	LOCK
LAST	LIKE	LONG
LAUGH	LIST	LOOK
LEAN	LIVE	LOOSEN
LEVEL	LOAD	LOVE
LICK		LOWER

12 REGULAR VERBS STARTING WITH "M"

MAIL
MAINTAIN
MANAGE
MARCH
MARK
MARRY

MATTER
MEASURE
MEMORIZE
MEND
MENTION
MERGE
MINE

MISS
MIX
MOURN
MOVE
MUG
MULTIPLY

13 REGULAR VERBS starting with "N", "O"

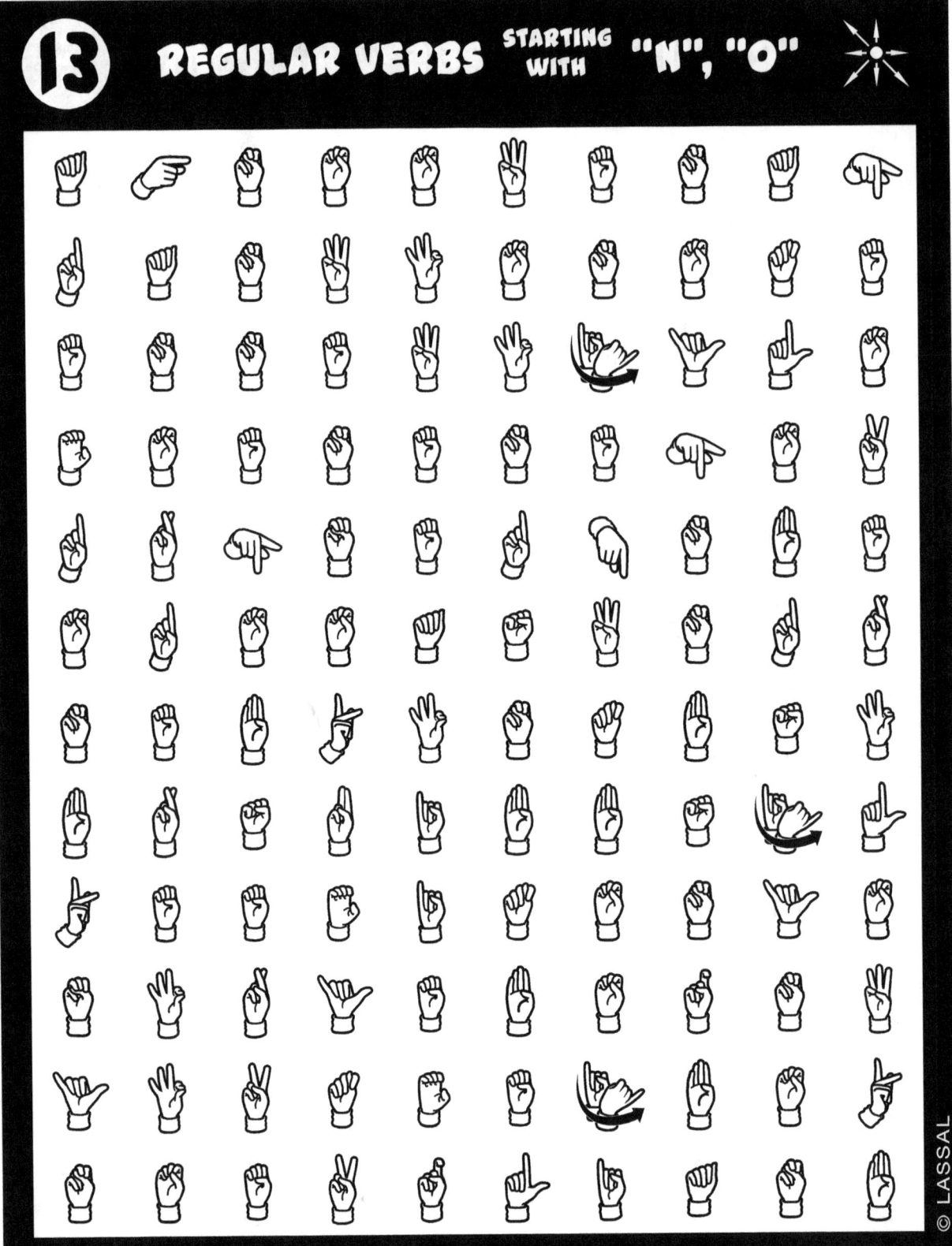

NAG	NOD	OFFER
NAIL	NOTE	OPEN
NAME	NOTICE	ORDER
NAP	OBEY	OVERFLOW
NEED	OBJECT	OWE
NEST	OBSERVE	OWN
	OFFEND	

14 REGULAR VERBS STARTING WITH "P"

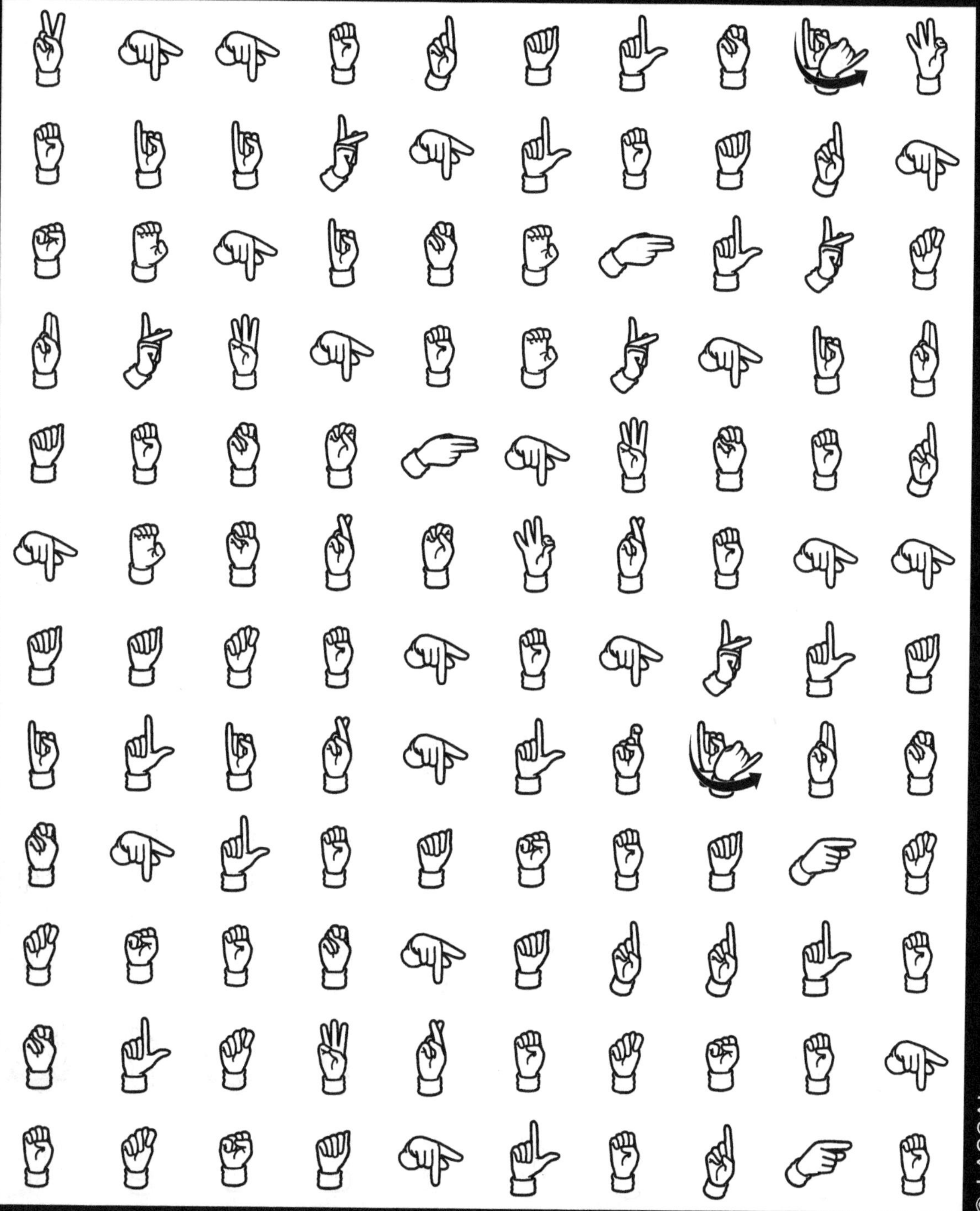

PADDLE	PECK	PET	PLANT
PAINT	PEDAL	PHONE	PLEAD
PANT	PEEL	PICK	PLEASE
PASTE	PERFORM	PINCH	PLEDGE
PAUSE	PERMIT	PLACE	PLUG
	PESTER	PLAN	

15. REGULAR VERBS starting with "P", "Q"

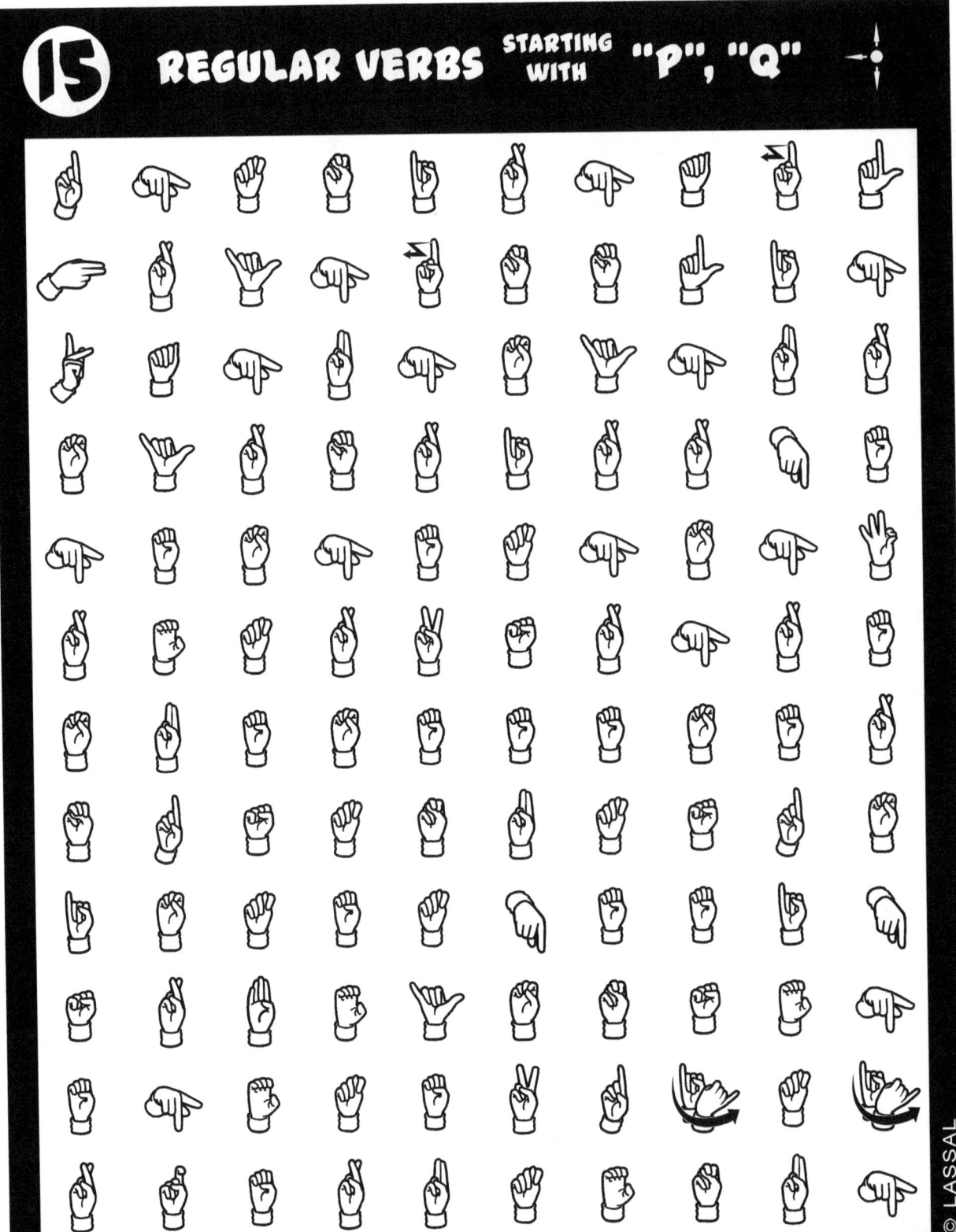

PRAY	PRINT	PRY
PREDICT	PRODUCE	PUMP
PREFER	PROMISE	PUNCTURE
PRETEND	PROPOSE	QUESTION
PREVENT	PROTECT	QUIZ
	PROTEST	

16 REGULAR VERBS STARTING WITH "R"

RADIATE	REALIZE	RELAX
RAISE	RECEIVE	RELEASE
RANT	REFUSE	REMAIN
RATE	REGRET	REMEMBER
REACH	REJECT	REMIND
	REJOICE	

17 REGULAR VERBS STARTING WITH "S"

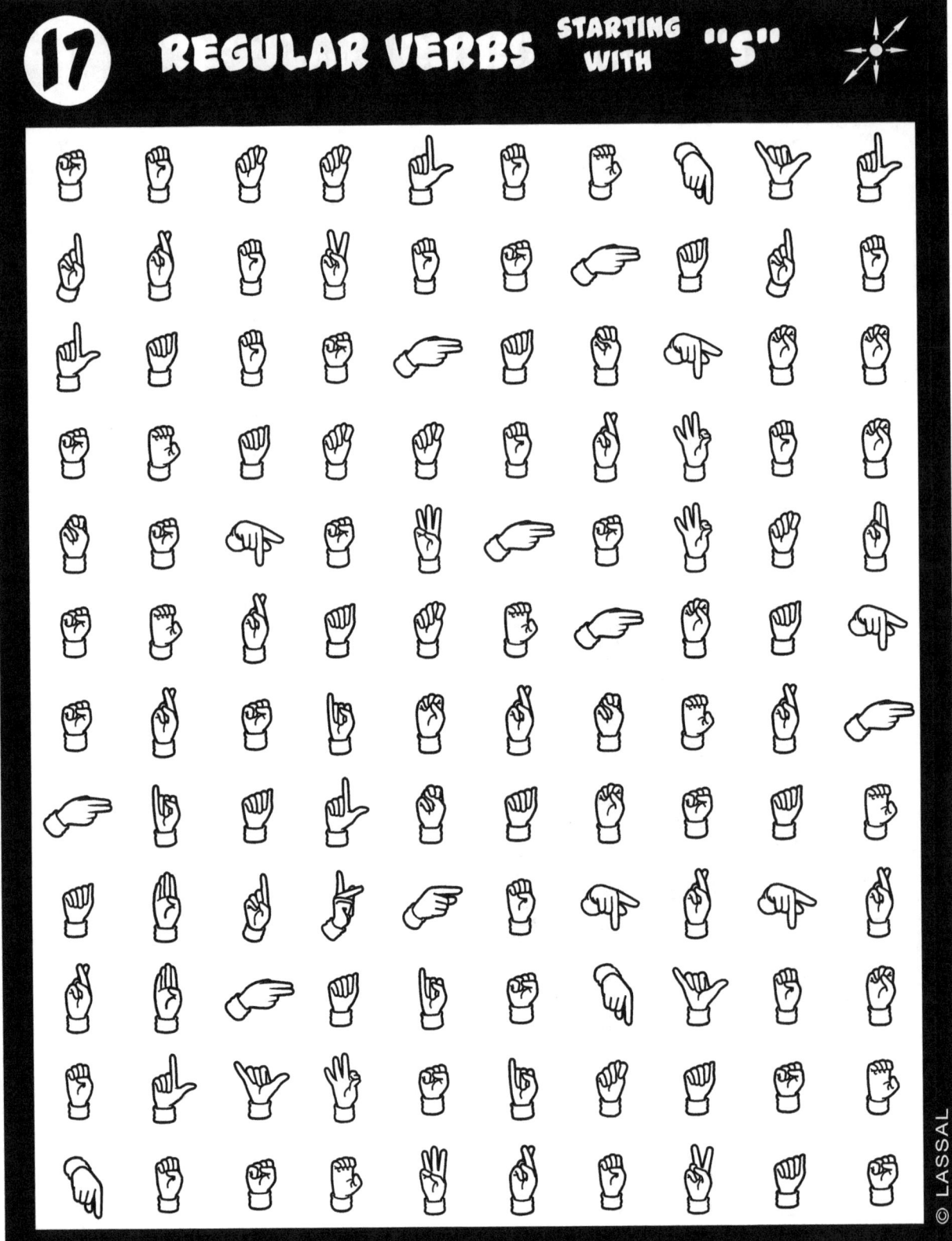

SAIL	SCATTER	SCRIBBLE	SEVER
SATISFY	SCOFF	SEAL	SHADE
SAVE	SCOLD	SEARCH	SHAMPOO
SAW	SCORCH	SEPARATE	SHARE
SCARE	SCRATCH	SETTLE	SIGN

18 REGULAR VERBS starting with "S"

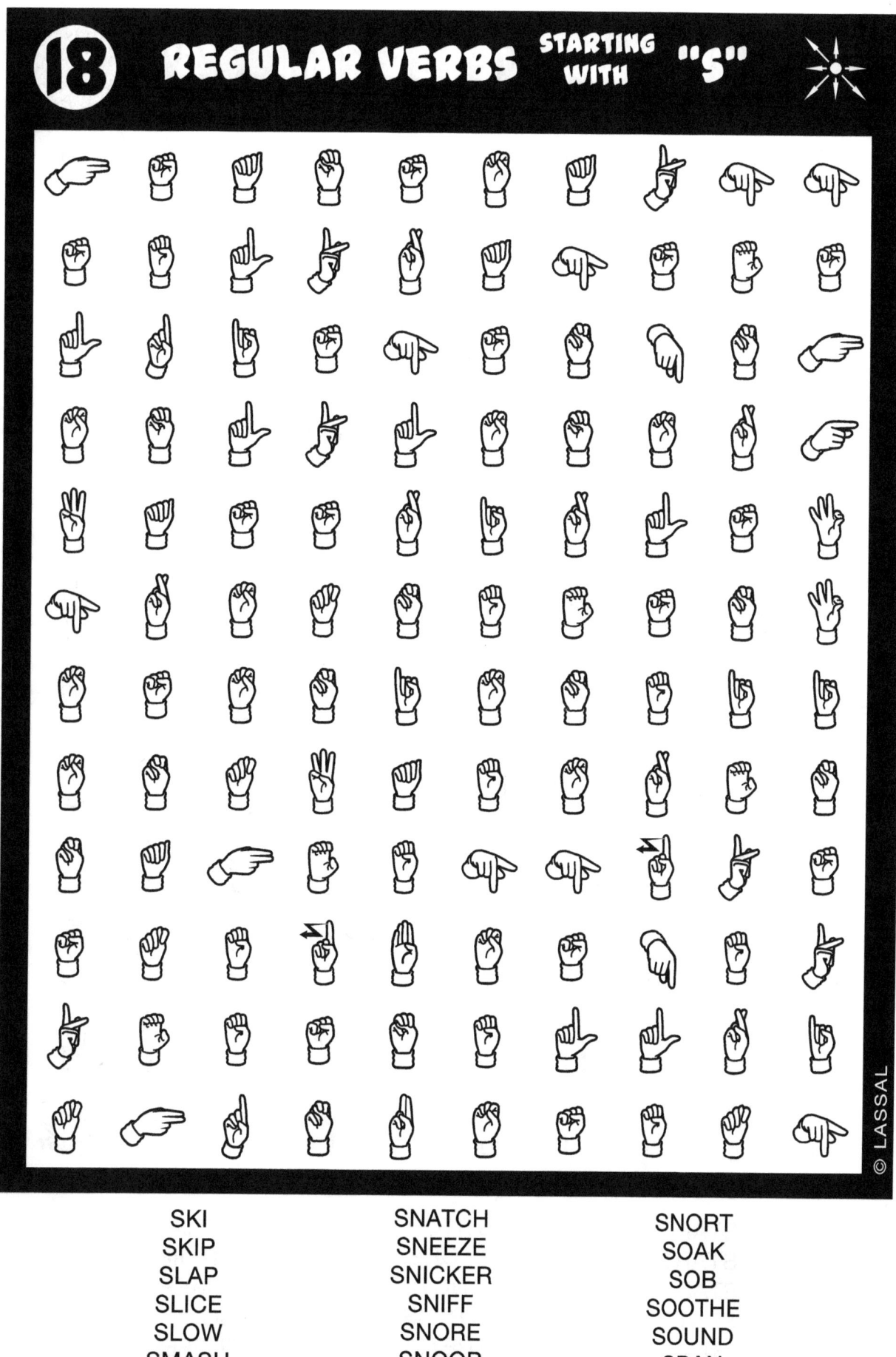

SKI	SNATCH	SNORT
SKIP	SNEEZE	SOAK
SLAP	SNICKER	SOB
SLICE	SNIFF	SOOTHE
SLOW	SNORE	SOUND
SMASH	SNOOP	SPAN
SMELL	SNOOZE	SPARKLE

19 REGULAR VERBS starting with "S"

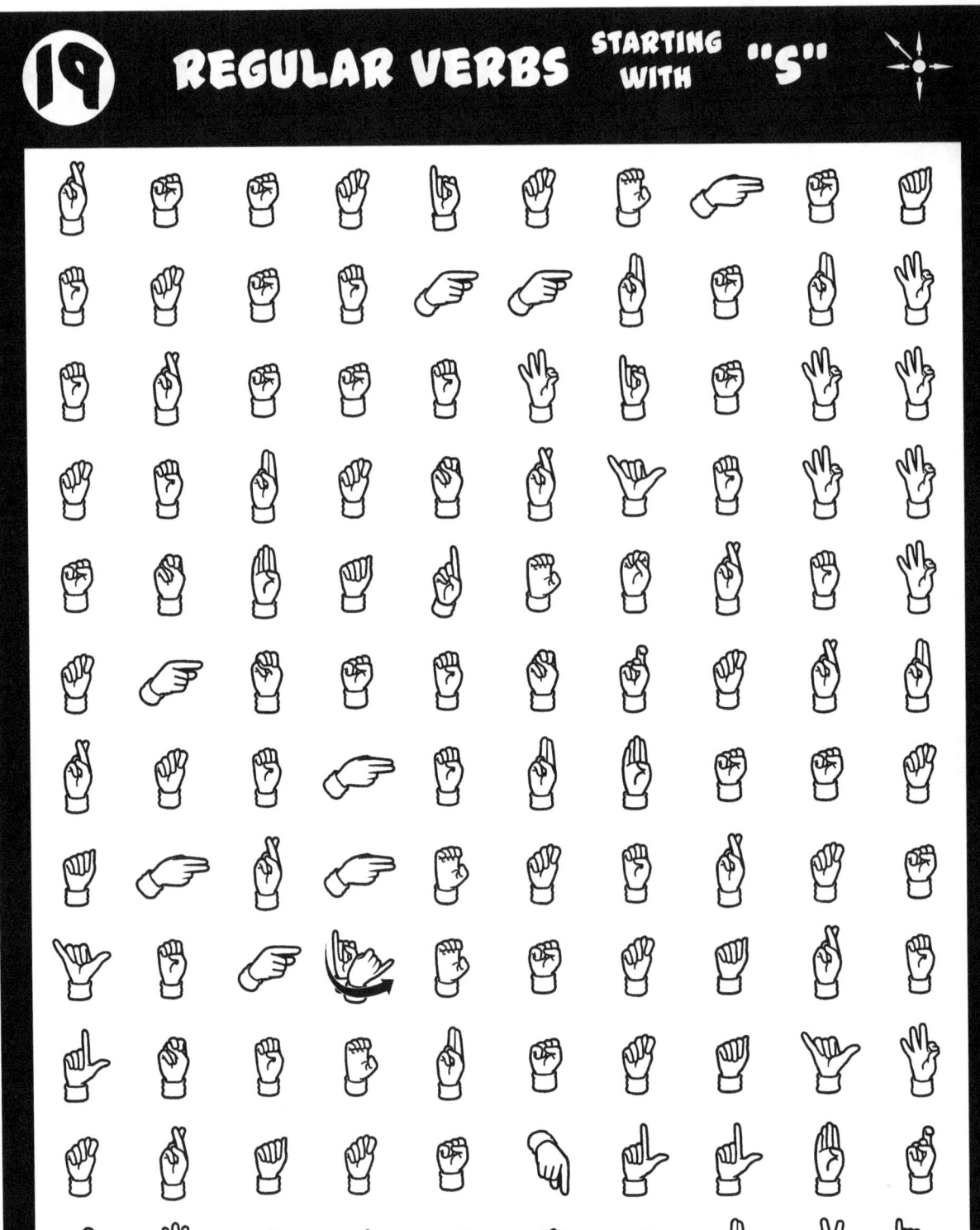

STARE	STITCH	STRAY
START	STORE	STUN
STASH	STRENGTHEN	SUBMERGE
STATE	STRESS	SUCCEED
STAY	STRETCH	SUFFER
STEER	STUFF	SUGGEST

20 REGULAR VERBS STARTING WITH "T"

TASTE
TAUNT
TEASE
TELEPHONE
TEMPT
TERRIFY

TEST
TESTIFY
THANK
THAW
THREATEN
THUNDER
TICKLE

TIE
TIME
TIRE
TOAST
TOSS
TOUCH

21 REGULAR VERBS STARTING WITH "T"

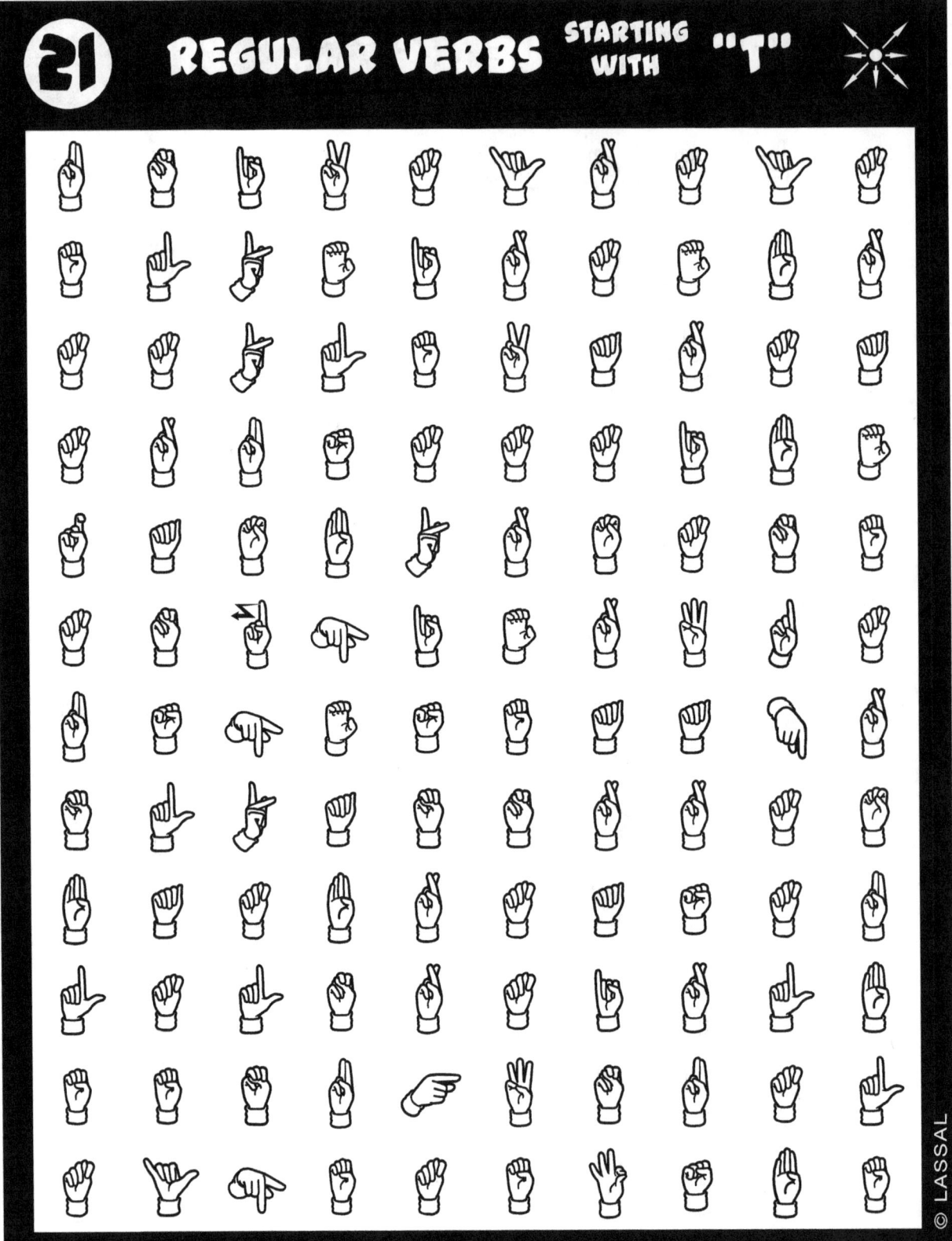

TOW	TRANSPORT	TROUBLE
TRACE	TRAP	TRUST
TRACK	TRAVEL	TRY
TRADE	TREMBLE	TUMBLE
TRAIN	TRICK	TWIST
TRANSLATE	TRICKLE	TYPE

REGULAR VERBS starting with "U"

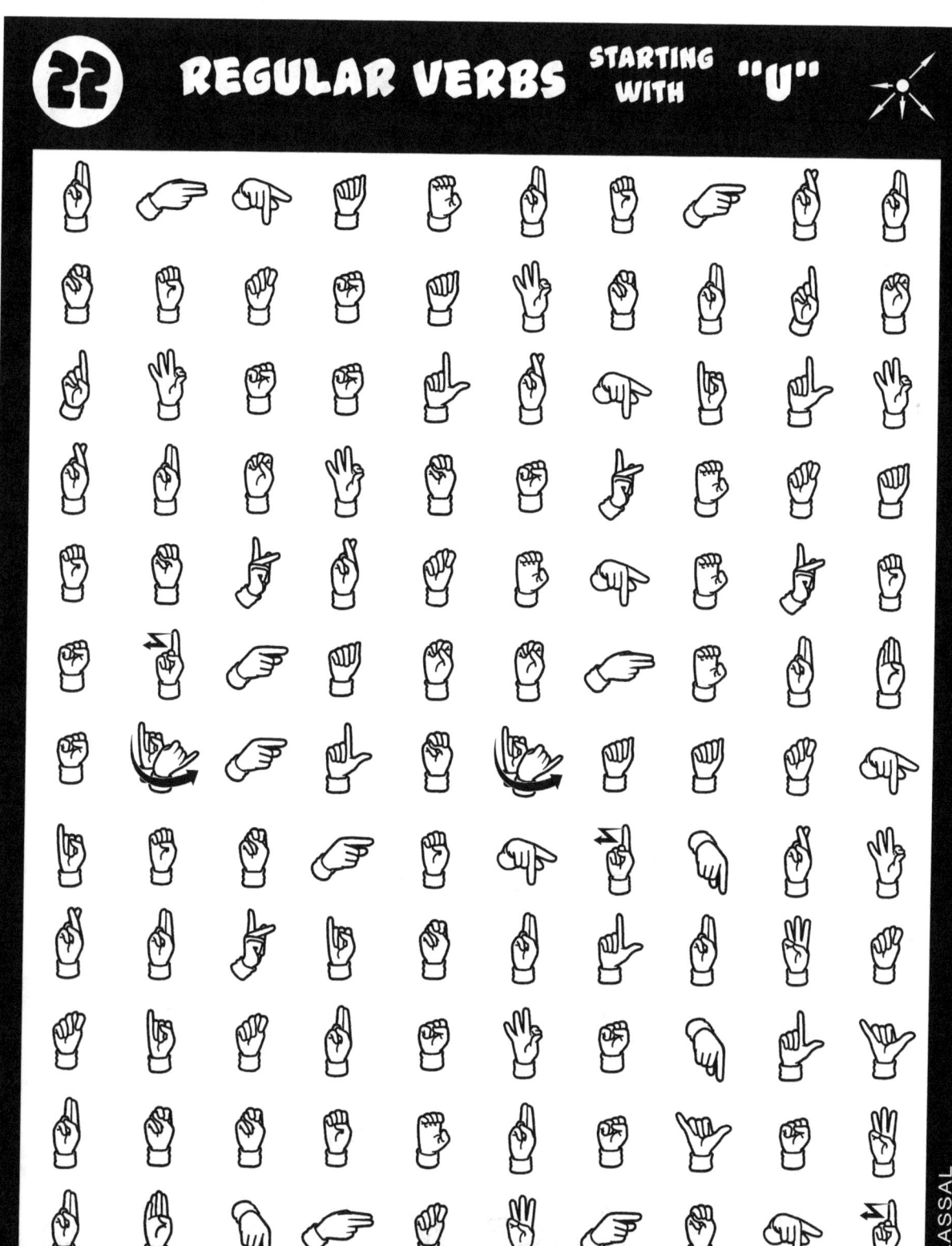

UNDRESS
UNFASTEN
UNITE
UNLOCK
UNPACK

UPSTAGE
URGE
UNTIE
USE
USURP

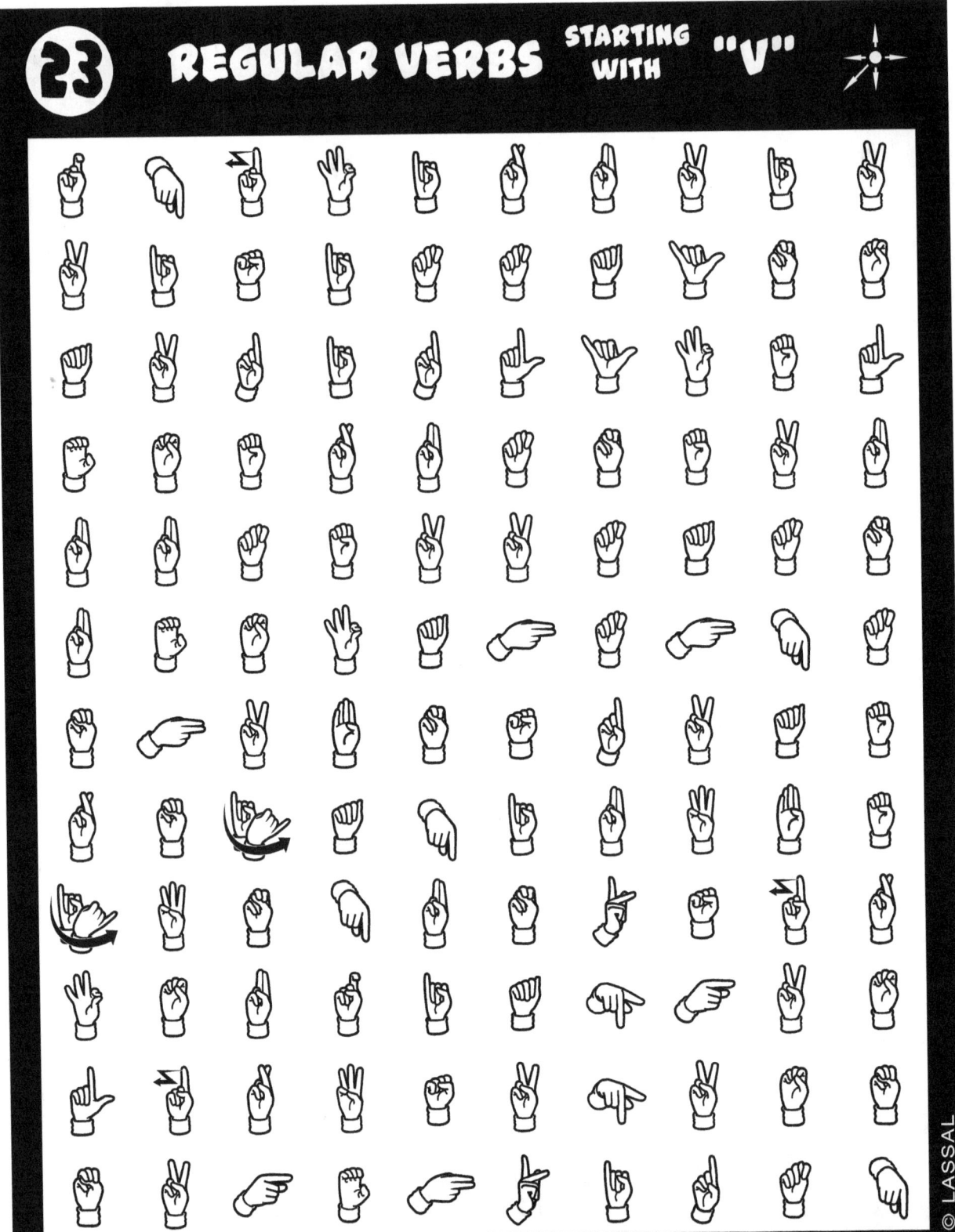

VACUUM
VALUE
VANISH

VANQUISH
VENTURE
VISIT

VOLUNTEER
VOTE
VOUCH

24 REGULAR VERBS STARTING WITH "W"

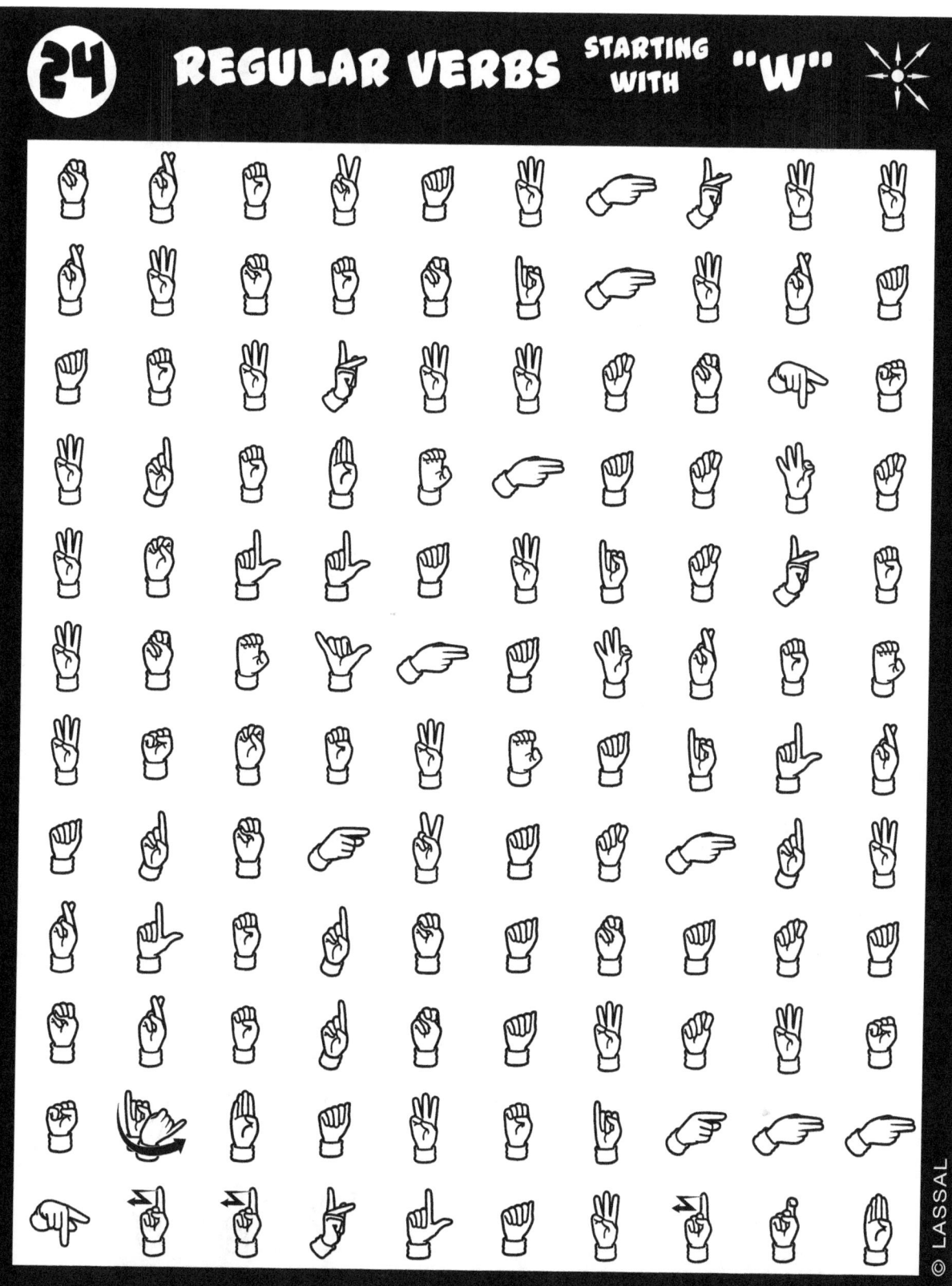

WAIT	WARN	WAVER
WALK	WASH	WED
WALLOW	WASTE	WEIGH
WANDER	WATCH	WELCOME
WANT	WATER	WHINE
WARM	WAVE	WHIRL

25 REG. VERBS STARTING WITH "W"-"Z"

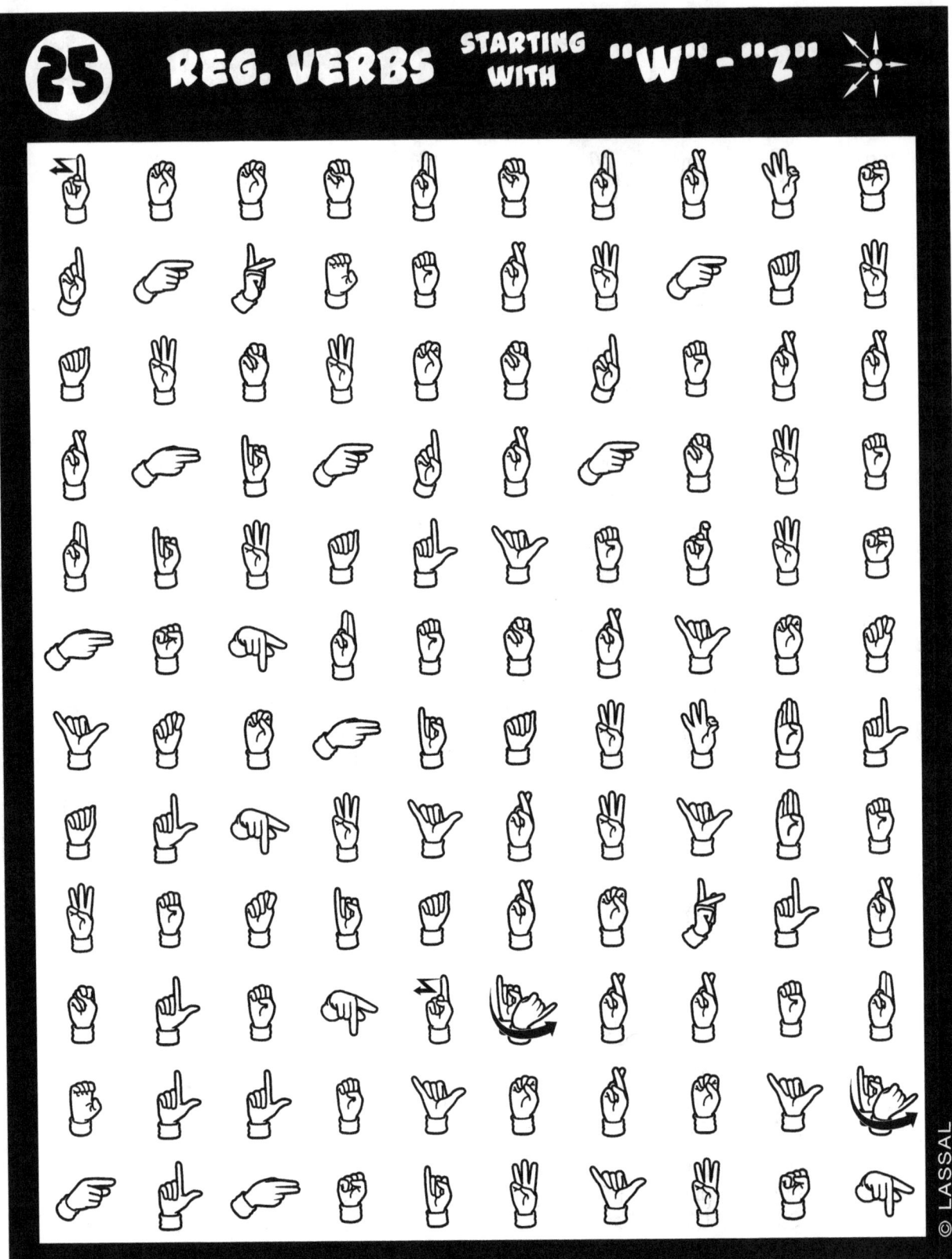

WHISTLE	WORK	XRAY
WINK	WORRY	YAWN
WIPE	WRAP	YELL
WISH	WRECK	YIELD
WOBBLE	WRESTLE	ZIP
WONDER		ZOOM

26 IRREG. VERBS STARTING WITH "A", "C", "D"

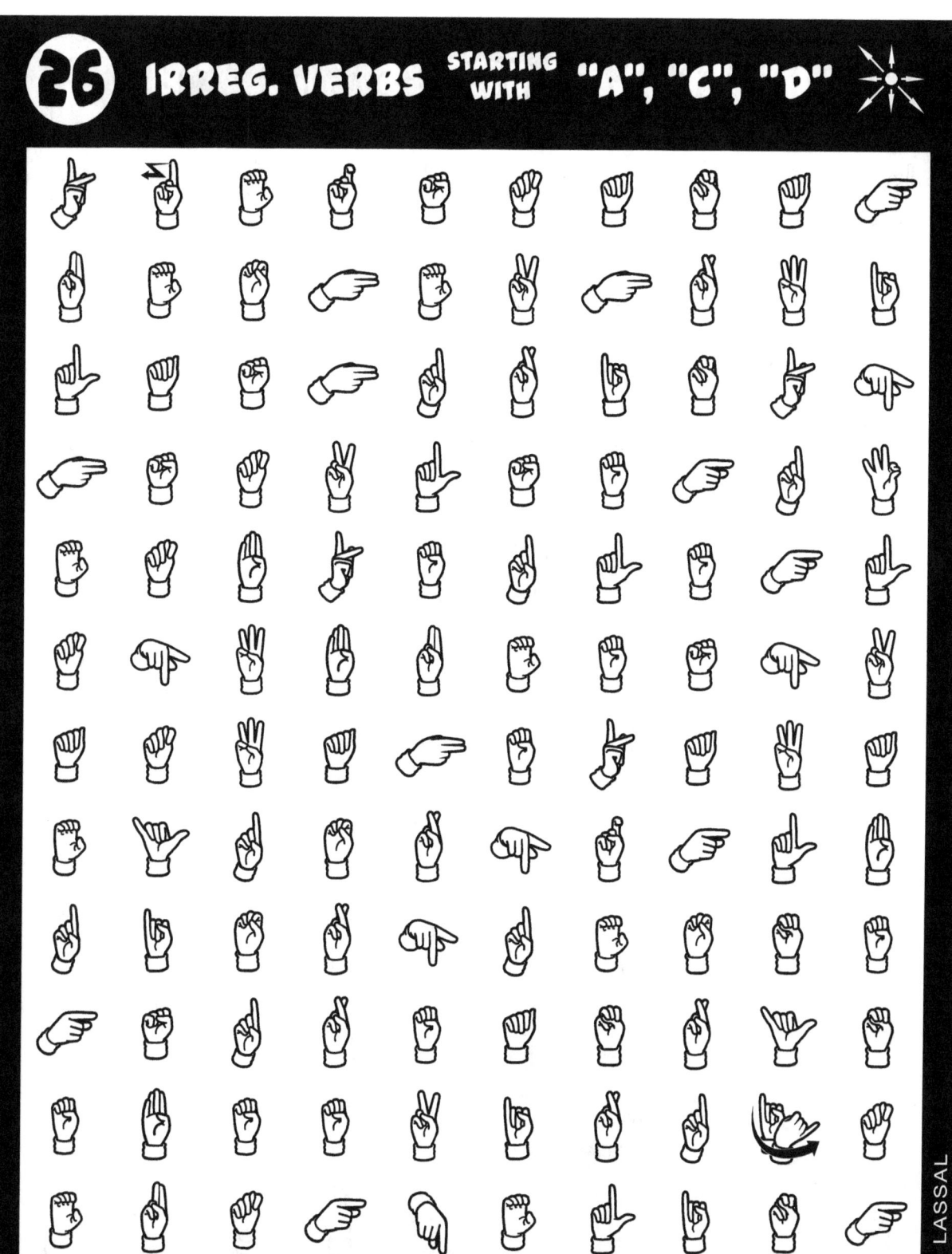

ARISE	COME	DIG
AWAKE	COST	DO
CAST	CREEP	DRAW
CATCH	CUT	DREAM
CHOOSE	DEAL	DRIVE
CLING		DRINK

27 IRREGULAR VERBS STARTING WITH "B"

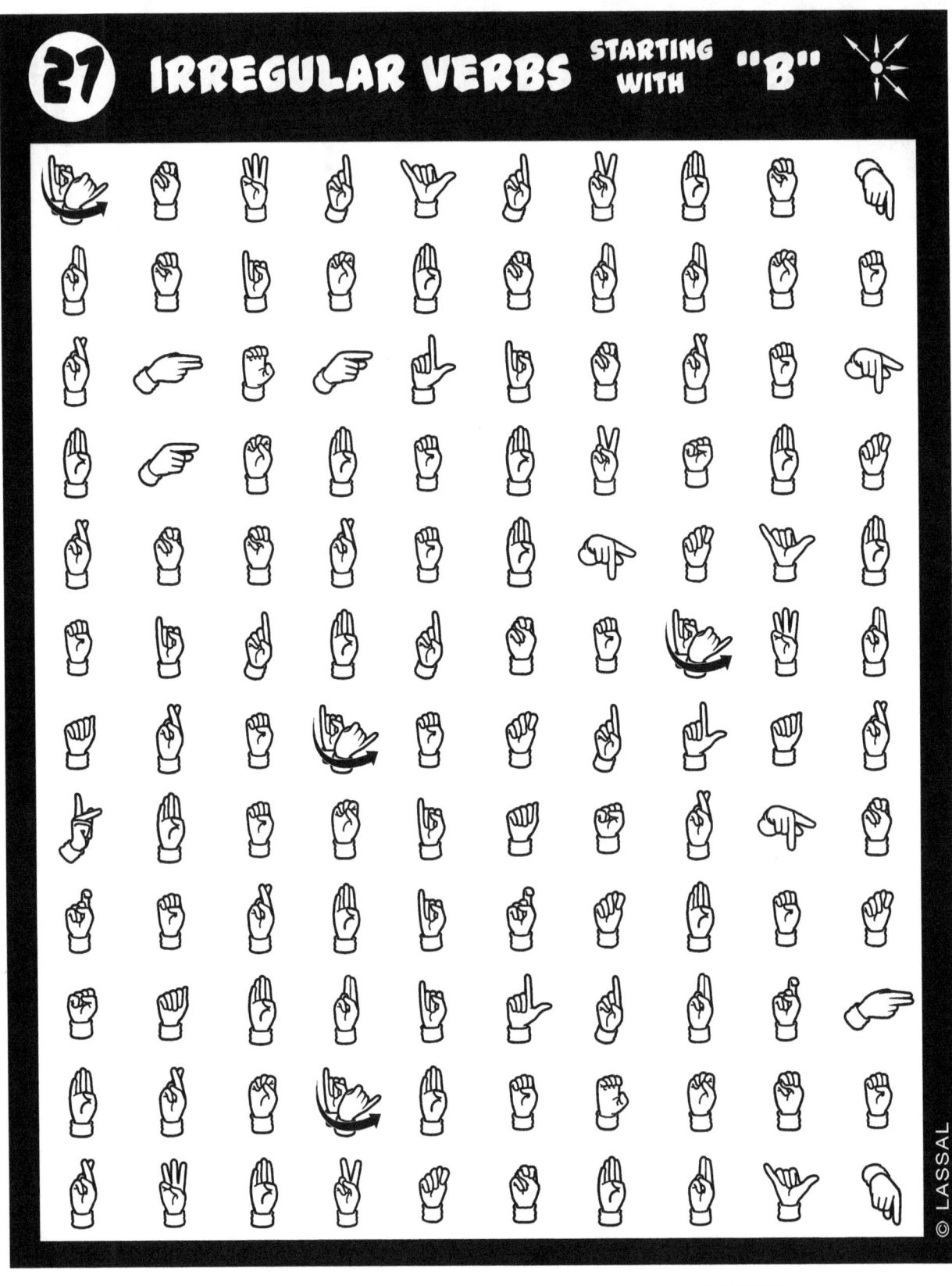

BE	BET	BREED
BEAR	BIND	BRING
BEAT	BITE	BUILD
BECOME	BLEED	BURN
BEGIN	BLOW	BURST
BEND	BREAK	BUY

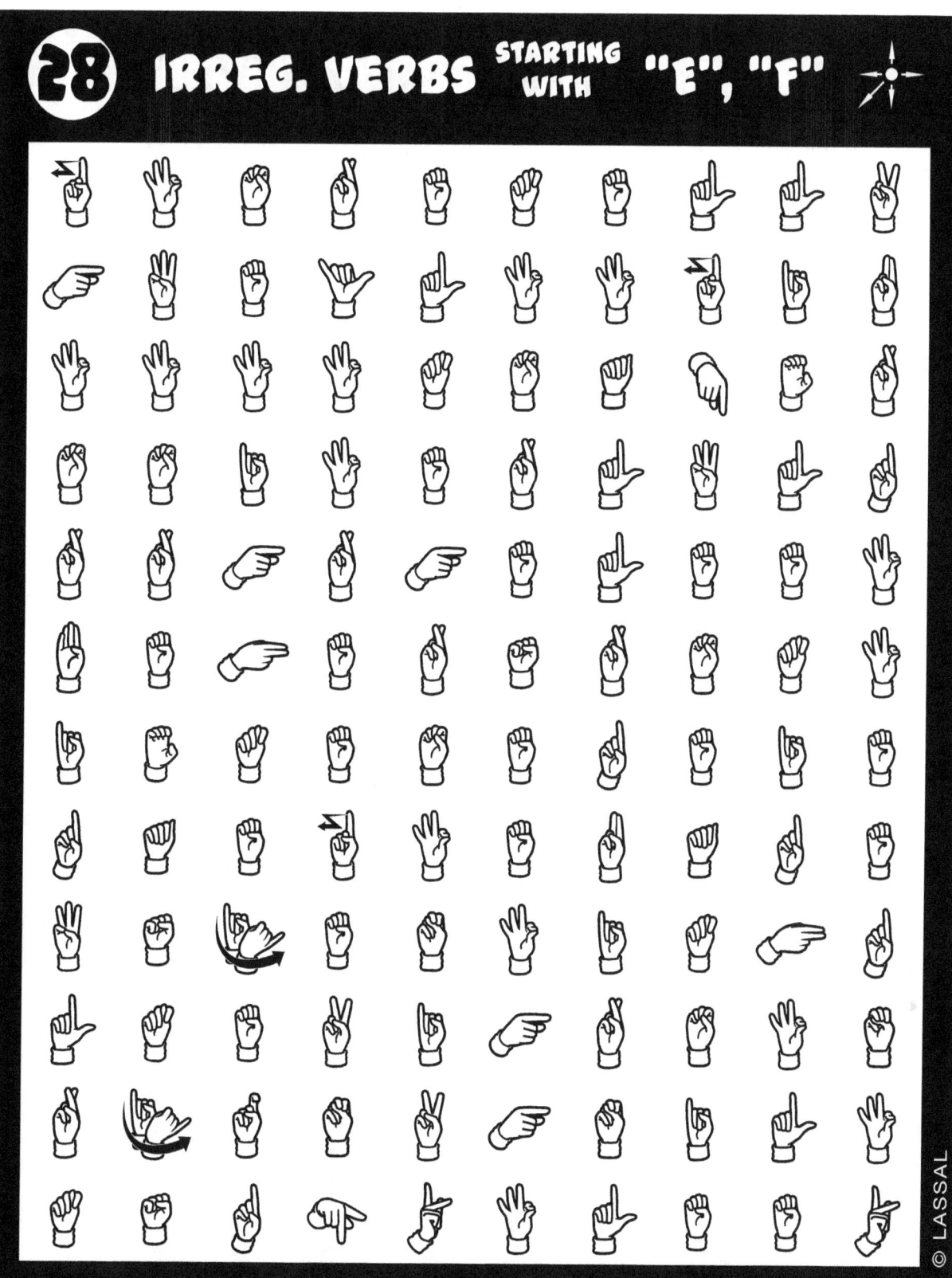

28 IRREG. VERBS STARTING WITH "E", "F"

EAT
FALL
FEED
FEEL
FIGHT
FIND
FLEE
FLING
FLY
FORBID
FORECAST
FORESEE
FORETELL
FORGET
FORGIVE
FREEZE

29 IRREG. VERBS STARTING WITH "G", "H", "I"

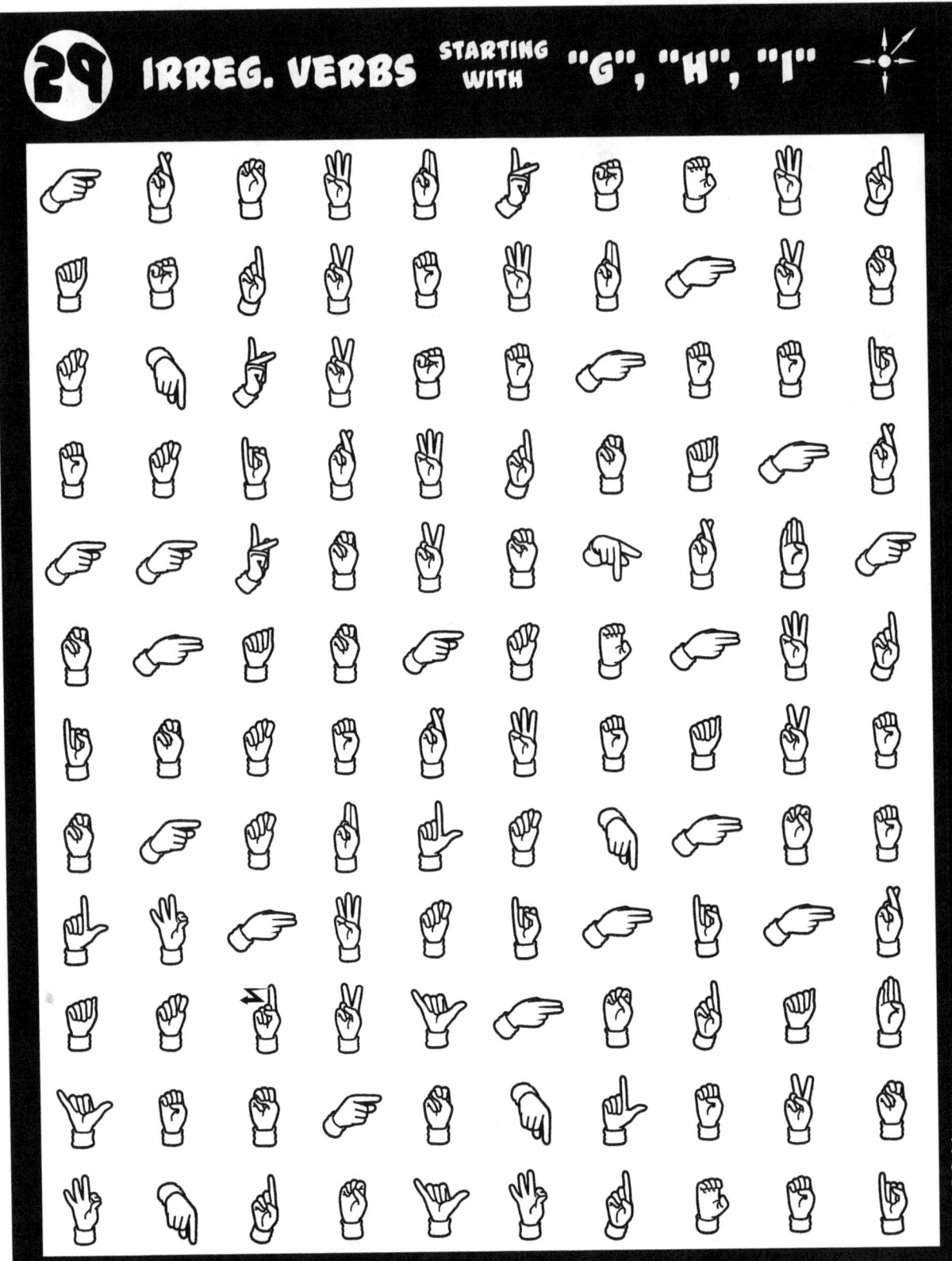

GET	HANDWRITE	HOLD
GIVE	HANG	HURT
GO	HAVE	INBREED
GRIND	HEAR	INLAY
GROW	HIDE	INTERWEAVE
	HIT	

30 IRREG. VERBS STARTING WITH "K", "L", "M"

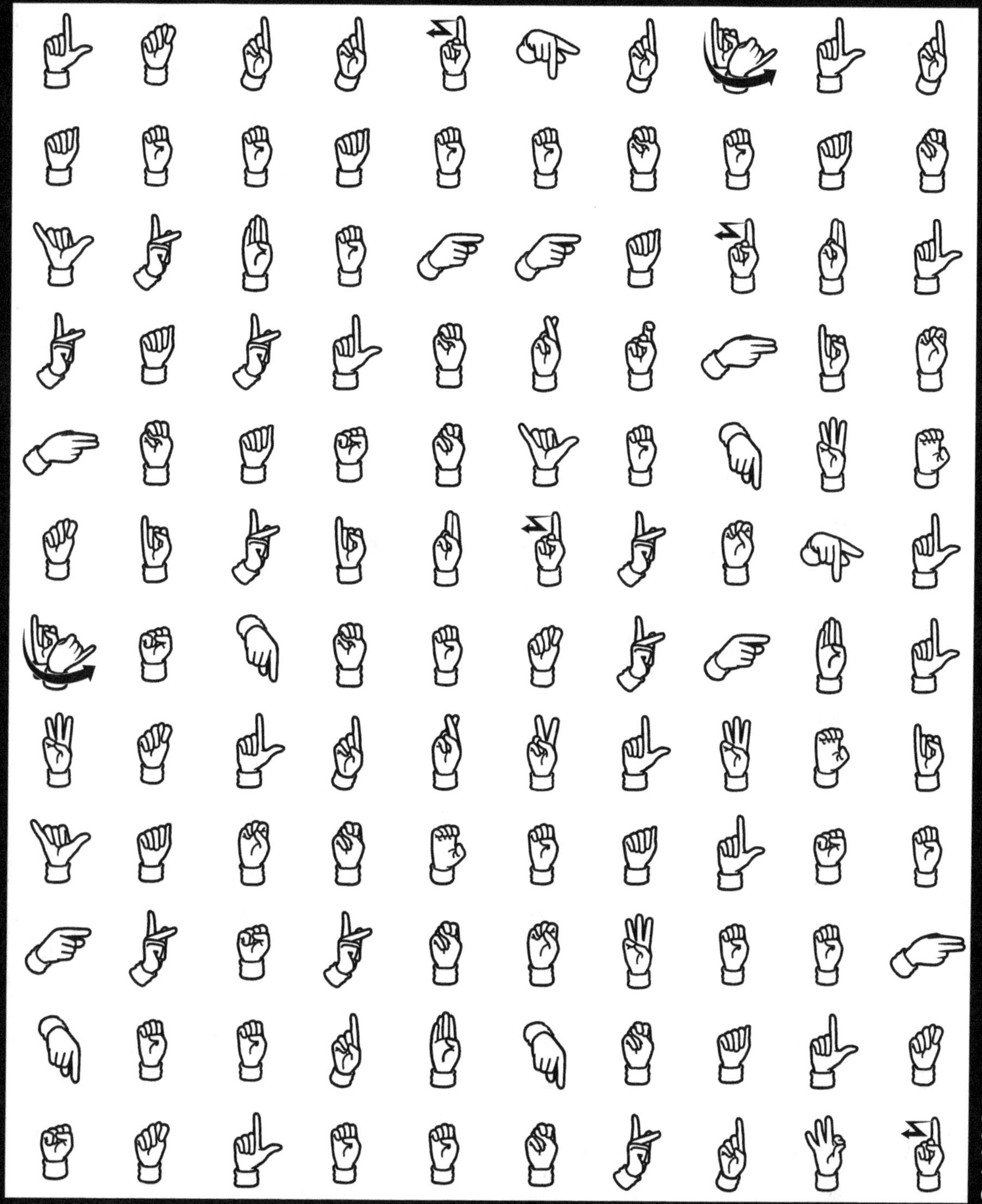

KEEP	LEARN	MAKE
KNEEL	LEAVE	MEAN
KNOW	LEND	MEET
LAY	LET	MISLEAD
LEAD	LIE	MISTAKE
	LOSE	

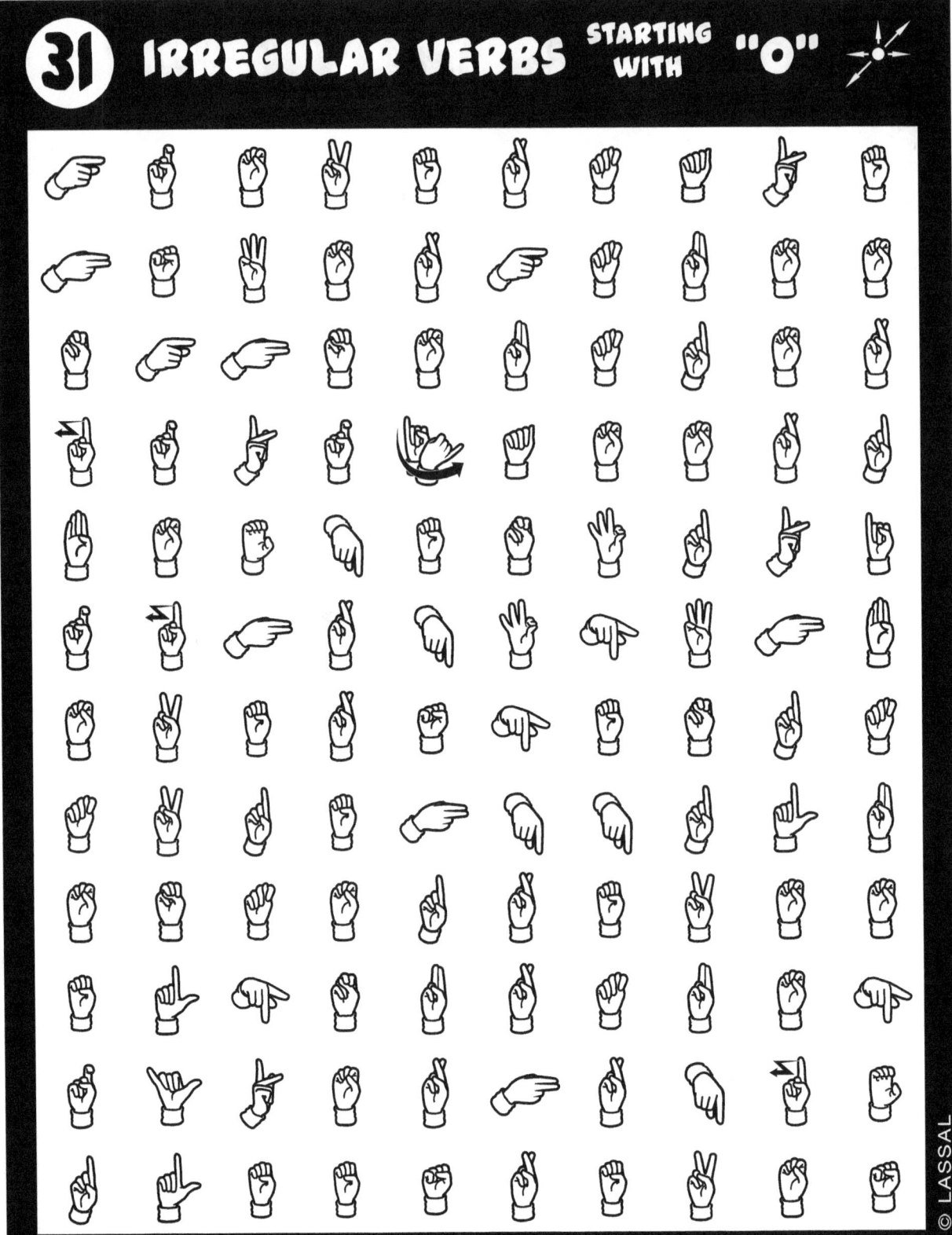

OFFSET
OUTBID
OUTDO
OUTGROW
OUTRUN
OVERDO
OVEREAT
OVERSEE
OVERSPEND
OVERTAKE

32. IRREG. VERBS STARTING WITH "P", "Q", "R"

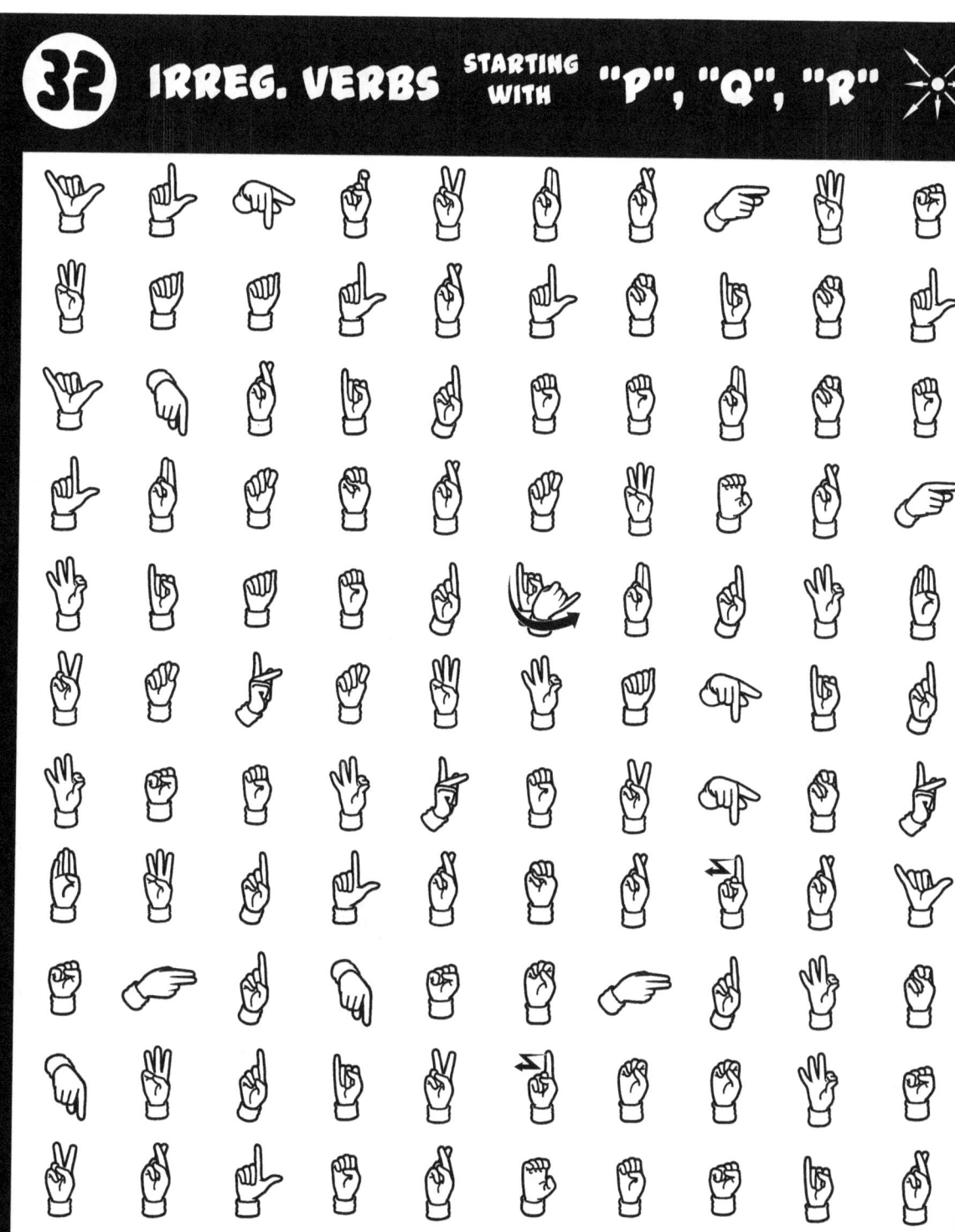

PARTAKE	QUIT	RIDE
PAY	READ	RING
PROVE	RID	RISE
PUT		RUN

33 IRREGULAR VERBS STARTING WITH "S"

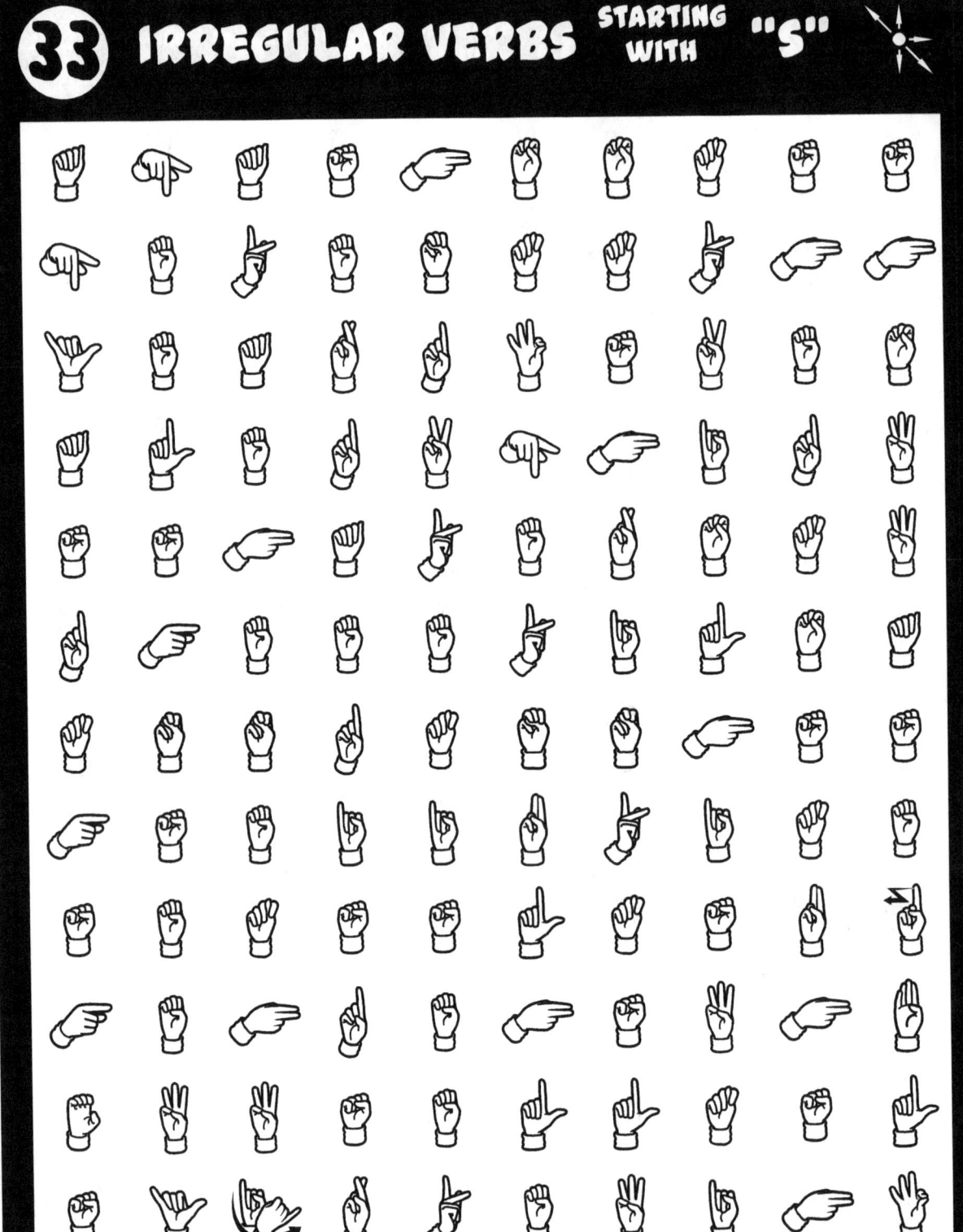

SAY	SEW	SHRINK
SEE	SHAKE	SHUT
SEEK	SHED	SING
SELL	SHOOT	SIT
SEND	SHOW	SLEEP
SET		SLIDE

34 IRREGULAR VERBS STARTING WITH "S"

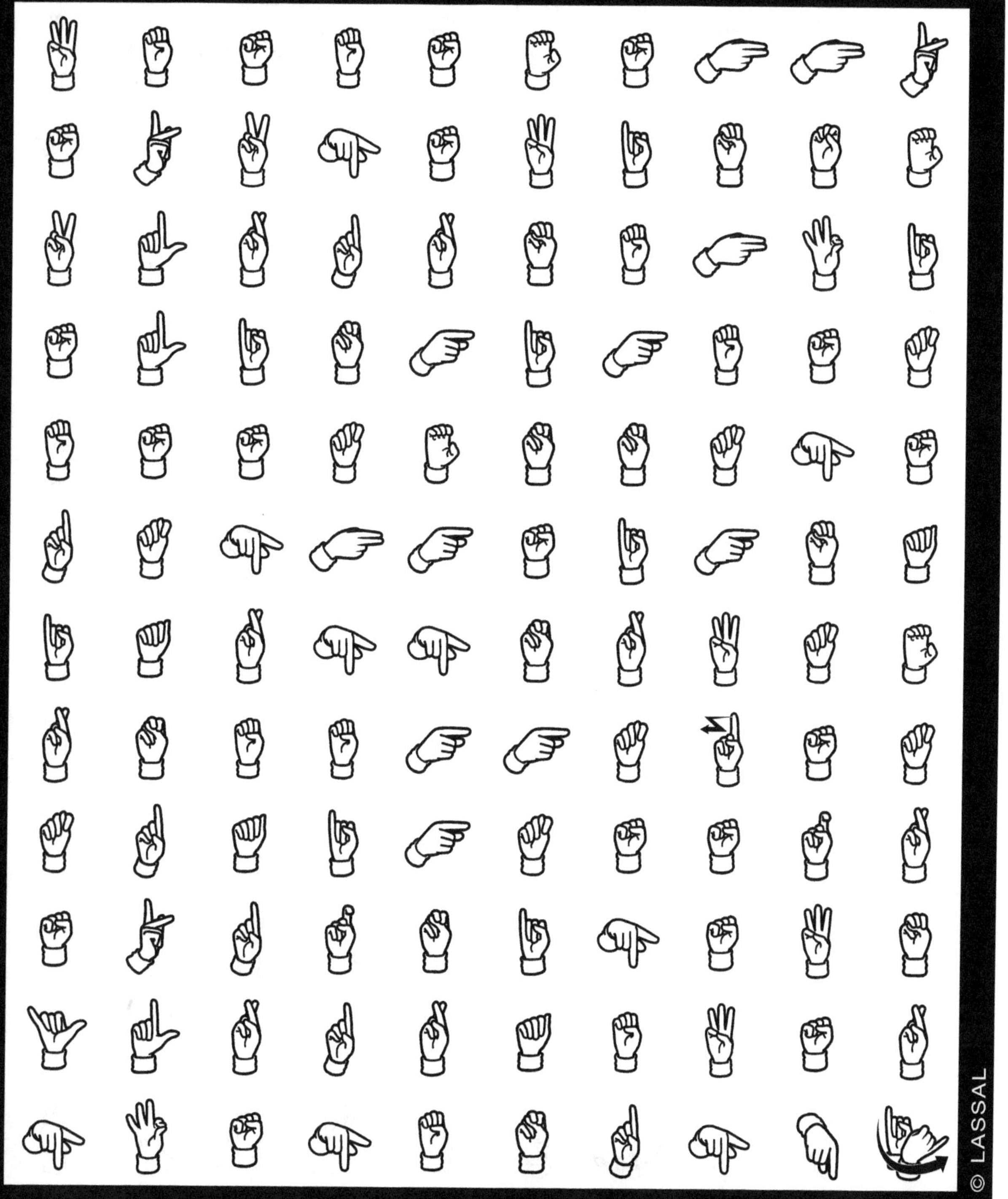

SLING	SPREAD	STRING
SLIT	SPRING	SWEAR
SPEAK	STAND	SWEEP
SPEND	STICK	SWIM
SPIN	STING	SWING
	STRIDE	

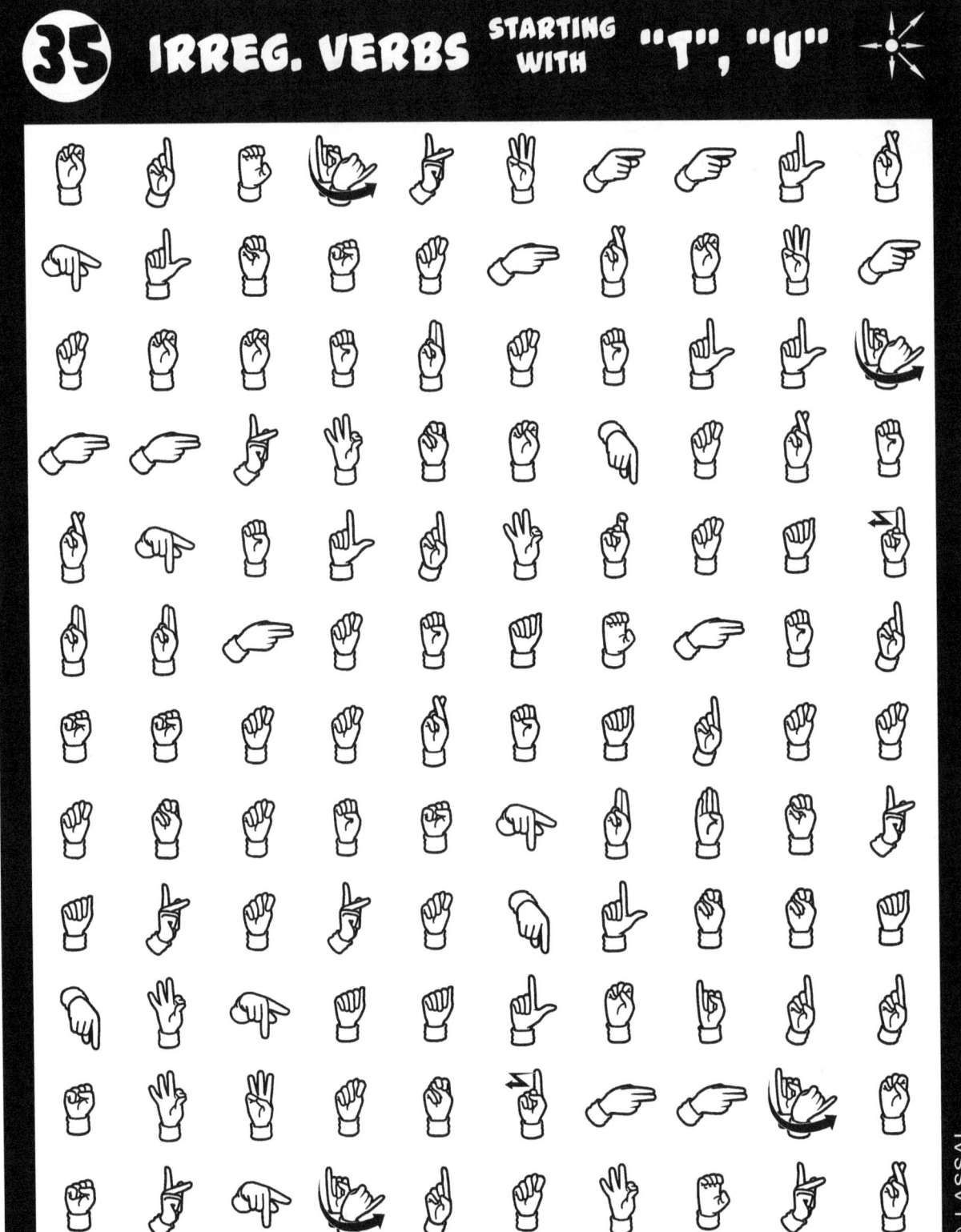

TAKE	THINK	UNDERSTAND
TEACH	THROW	UNDO
TEAR	THRUST	UPHOLD
TELL	TREAD	UPSET

36 IRREGULAR VERBS STARTING WITH "W"

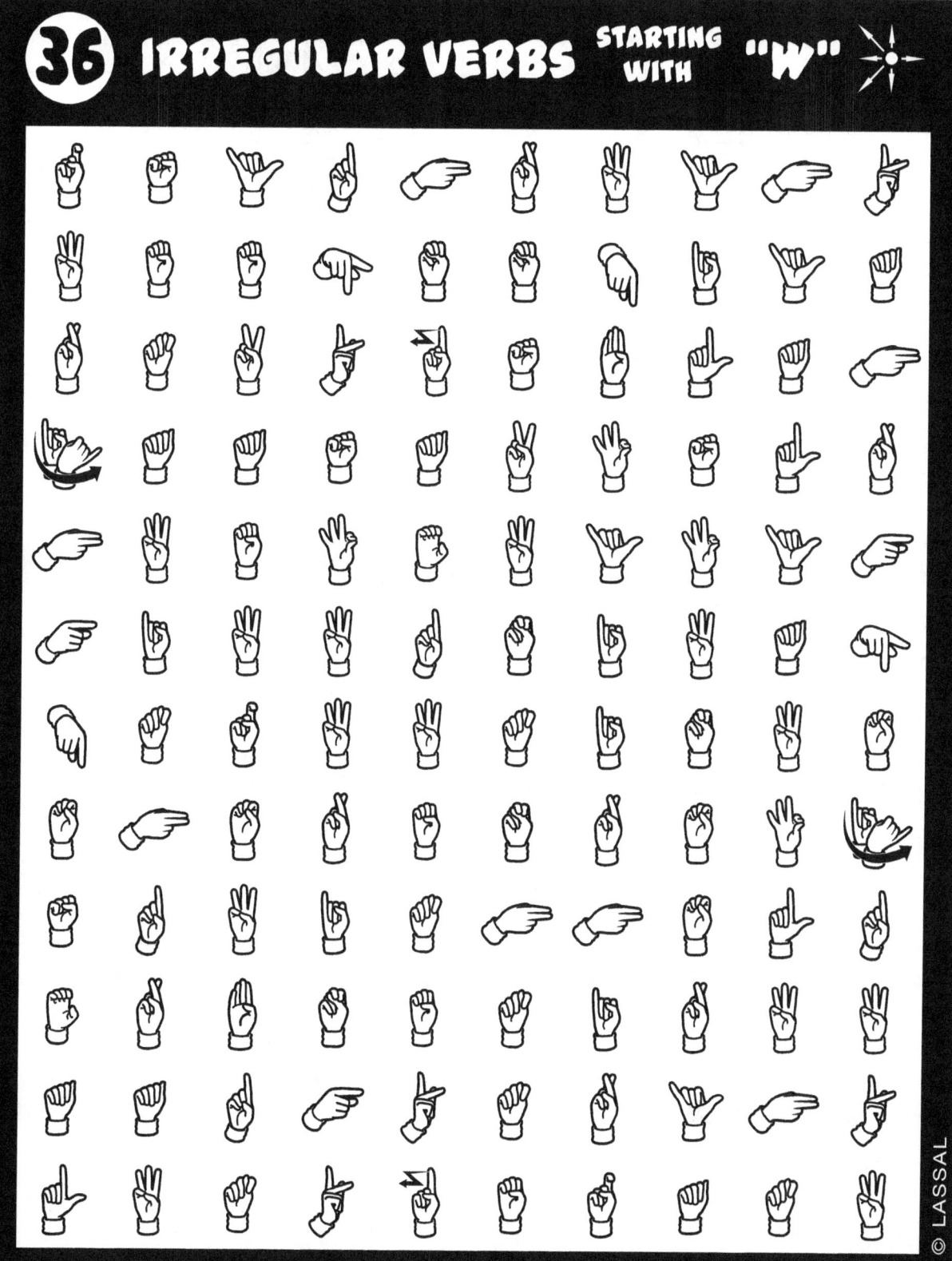

WAKE
WAYLAY
WEAR
WEAVE
WEEP
WET
WIN
WIND
WITHDRAW
WITHHOLD
WRING
WRITE

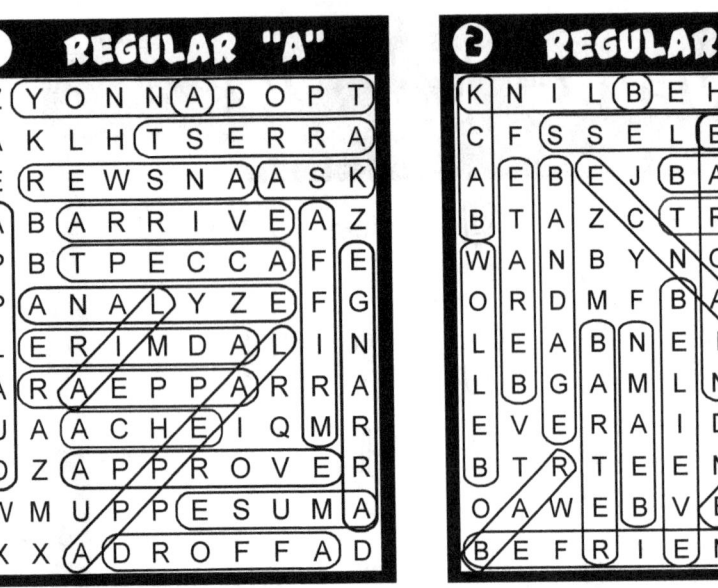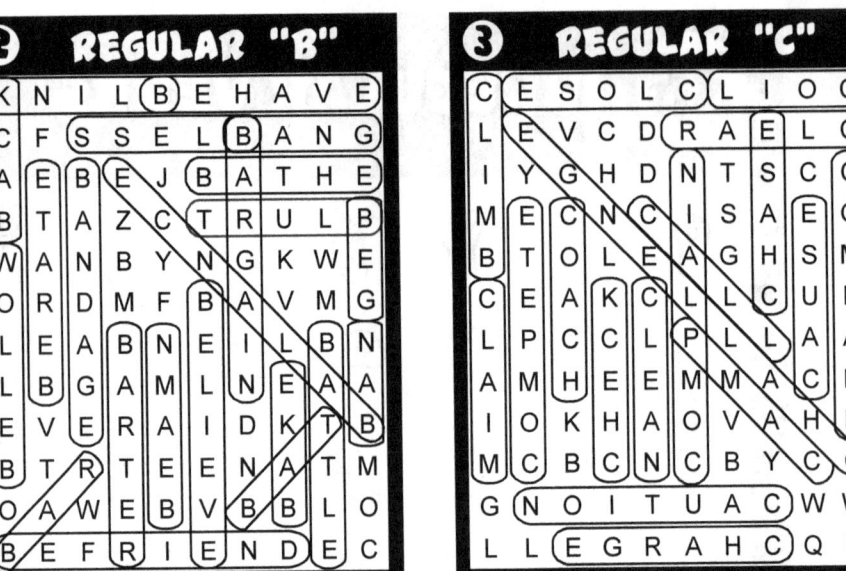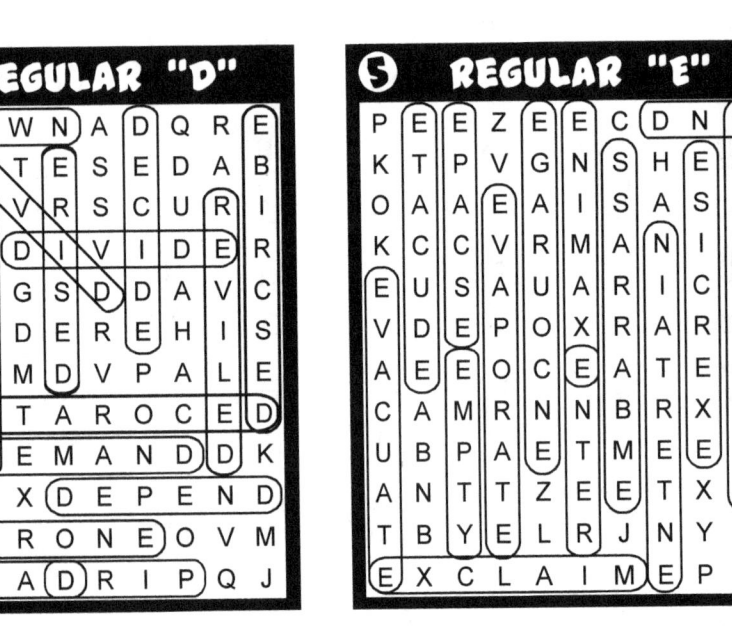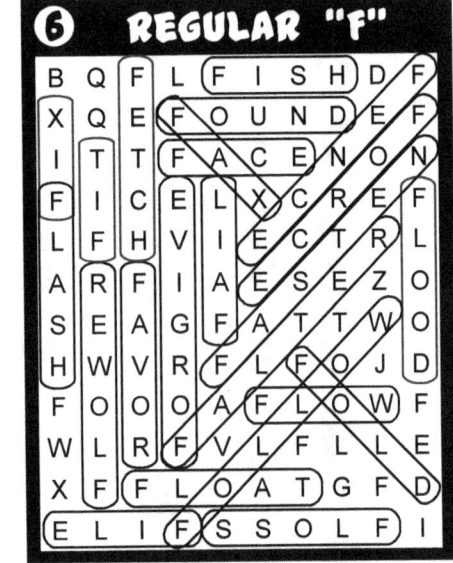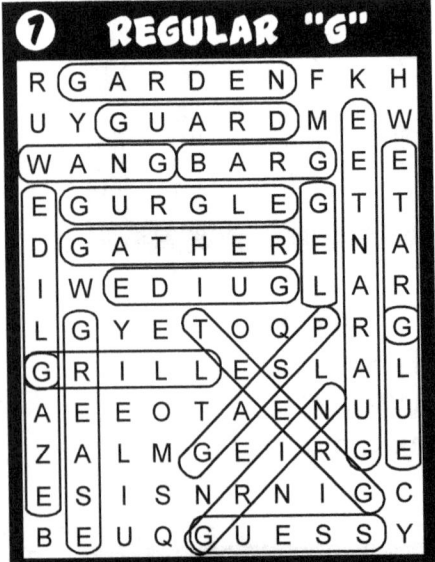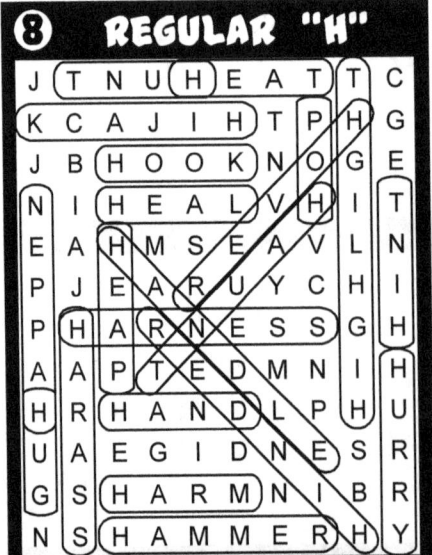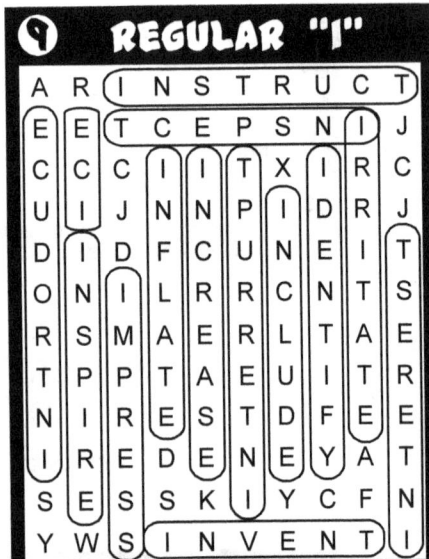

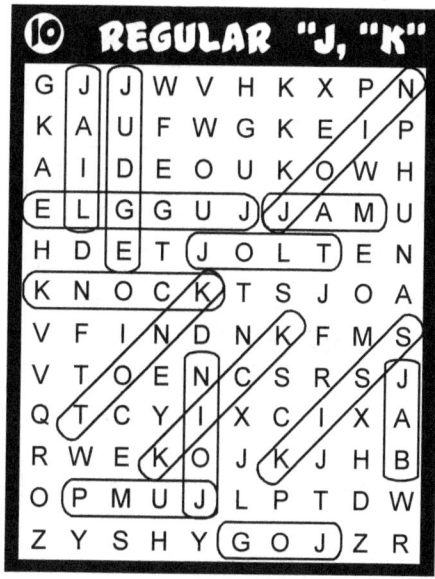
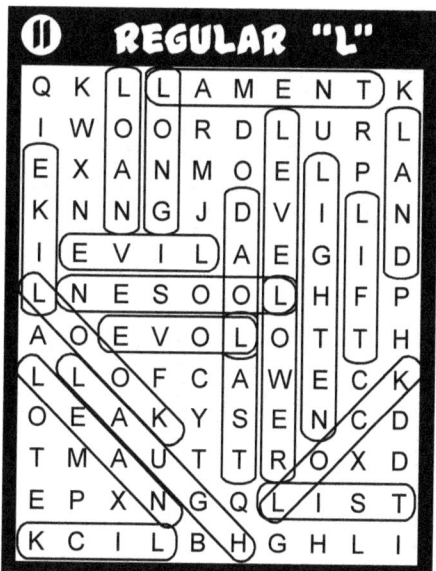
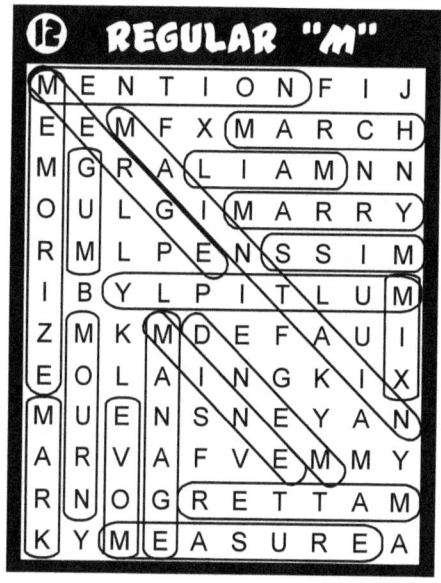
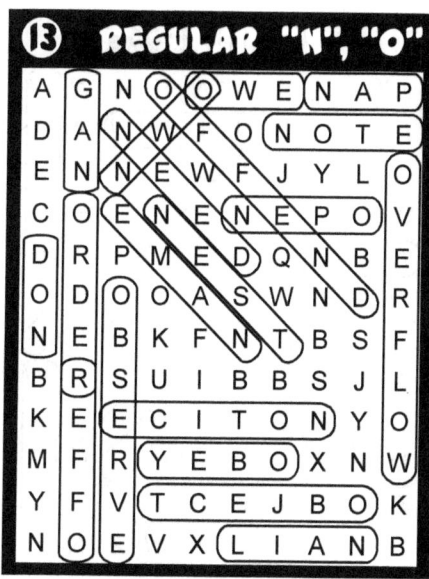
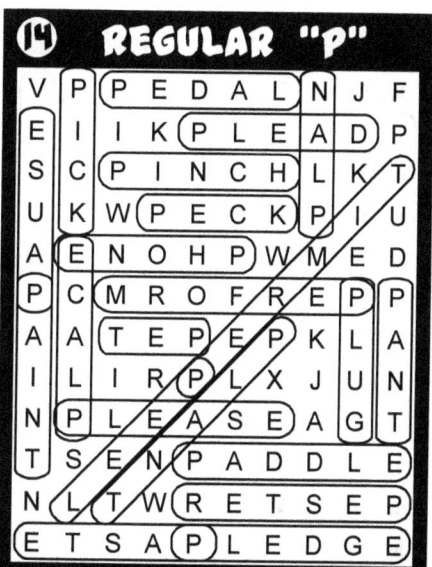

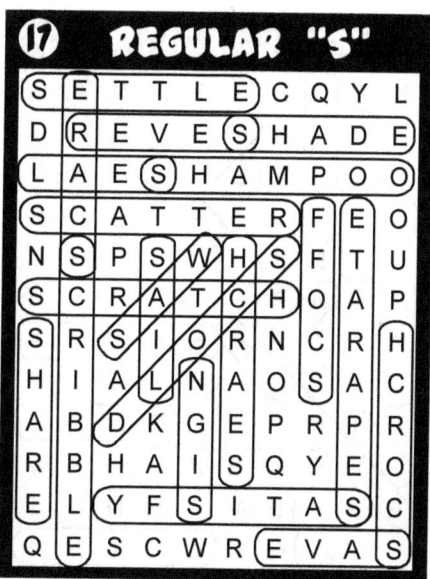
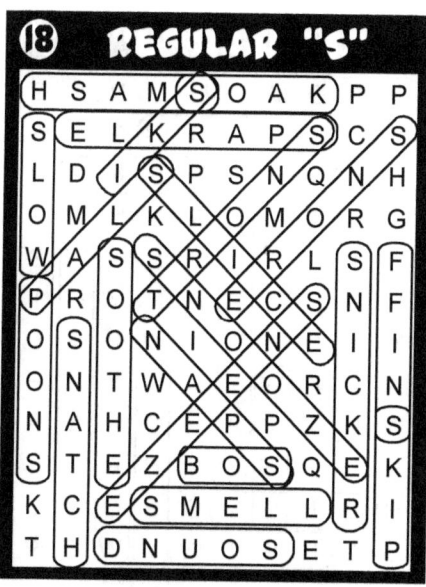

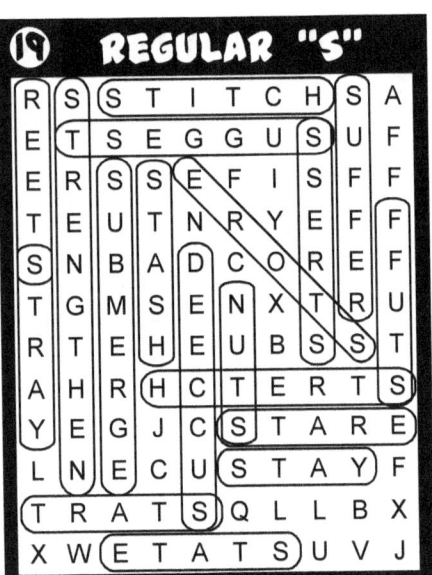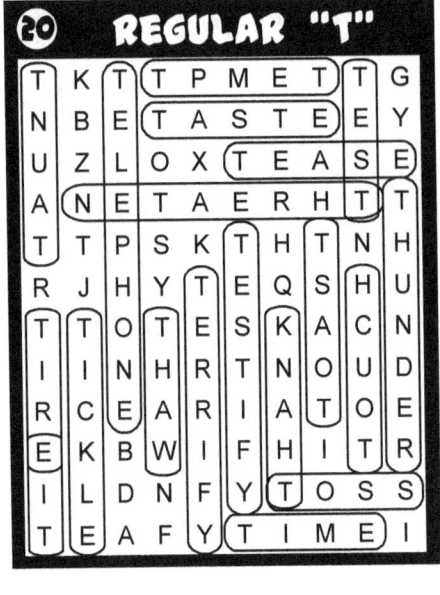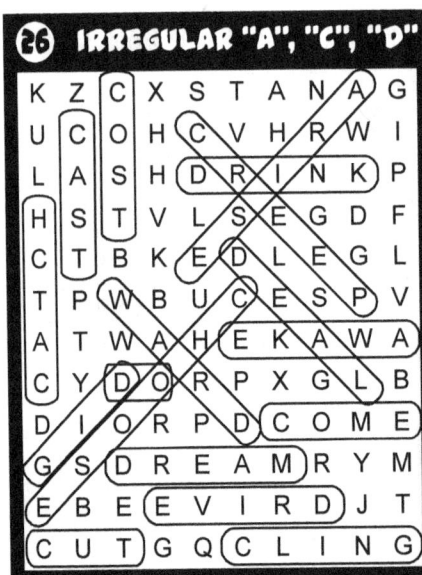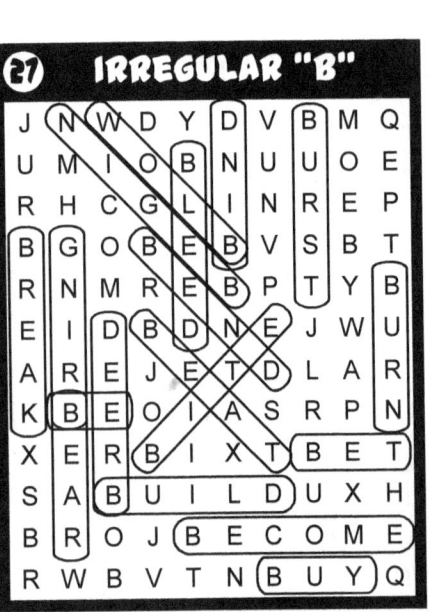

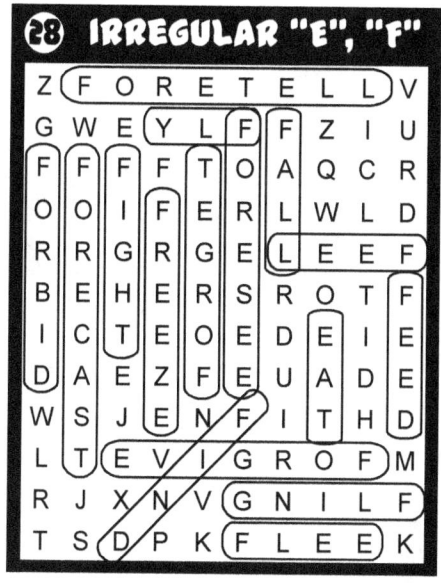

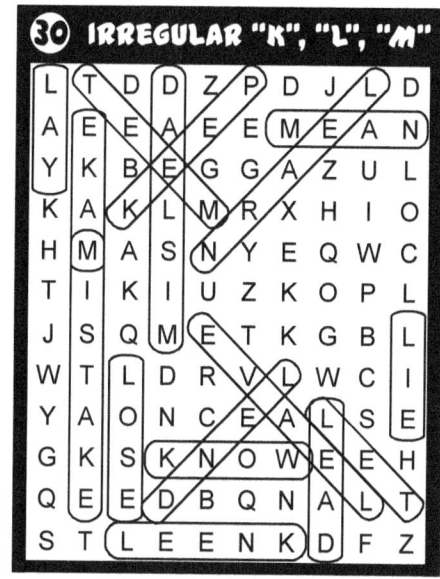
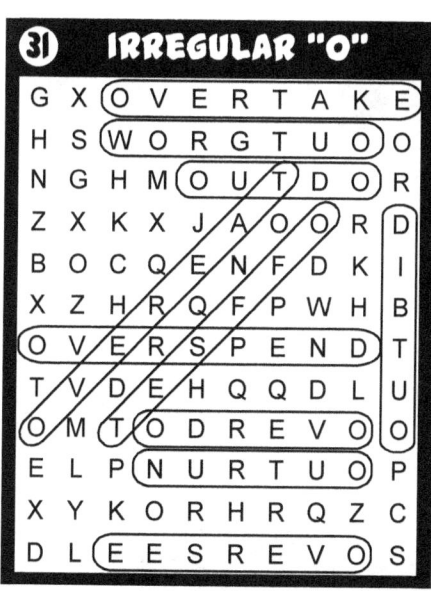

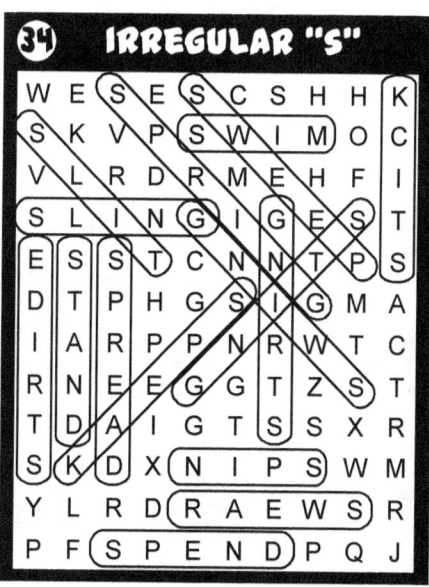
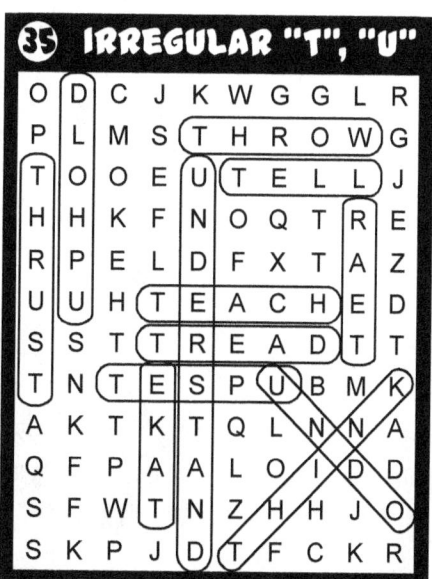
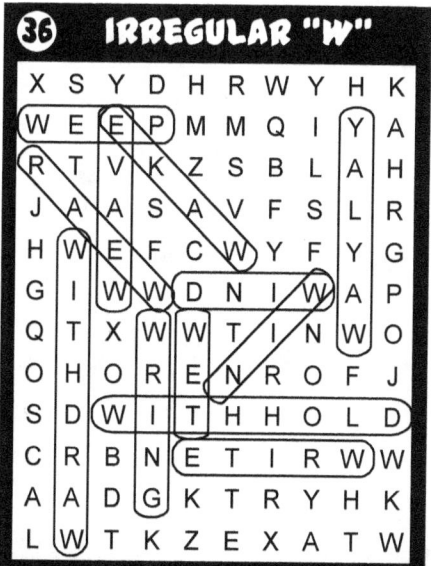

FINGER ALPHABET COOL KIDS
36 WORD SEARCH PUZZLES
WITH THE
AMERICAN **SIGN** LANGUAGE ALPHABET

NEW

HAVE FUN & LEARN
ADJECTIVES
3RD - 5TH GRADE

ISBN 978-3-86469-104-1

SOON AVAILABLE FOR
COOL ADULTS

FINGER ALPHABET COOL KIDS
WORD SEARCH PUZZLES 36

WITH THE
AMERICAN **SIGN** LANGUAGE ALPHABET

HAVE FUN & LEARN
ADVERBS
3RD - 5TH GRADE

ISBN 978-3-86469-108-9

SOON AVAILABLE FOR
COOL ADULTS

www.ingramcontent.com/pod-product-compliance
Lightning Source LLC
Chambersburg PA
CBHW081024040426
42444CB00014B/3335